THE CELL BLOCK PRESENTS…

CALIFORNIA PRISON STORIES

Published by: THE CELL BLOCK™

THE CELL BLOCK
P.O. Box 1025
Rancho Cordova, CA 95741

Instgram.com/mikeenemigo
Facebook.com/thecellblockofficial

Copyright© 2021 Mike Enemigo

Cover design by Mike Enemigo

Send comments, reviews, or other business
inquiries:
info@thecellblock.net
Visit our website: thecellblock.net

GEORGE

California prison officials consider him to be the most dangerous prisoner they've ever housed. His name still strikes fear in prison authorities, even fifty years after his murder; and not just in California, but prisons across the nation, as even in death they fear his influence. Who is he? George Lester Jackson, prison number A63837, and this is his story.

$$$$$

Jackson's family moved from Chicago to California in 1956, when he was 15 years old. A year later, he was arrested for petty theft and spent seven months in the California Youth Authority.

In 1960, Jackson was arrested again, this time charged with second-degree armed robbery for robbing a Los Angeles gas station for $70; he pled guilty. In Jackson's letters to family and friends, he claimed to be innocent of the crime, but says he pled guilty because he was promised a "short county jail term." However, the sentencing judge, taking into account his previous convictions, instead sentenced him to state prison for a term of "one year to life."

With this sentence, Jackson reasonably expected to be out in a year or two. After all, the crime was relatively petty, meaning no one got hurt. All Jackson would have to do is stay out of trouble so prison officials would document such. He was hopeful about getting out of prison, as he expressed in earlier letters to family members. He wrote about wanting better shoes so he could take care of his feet, which were sore, and he asked his father, a postal worker, to help him get a job once released. In an effort to remain trouble-free, he even avoided participating in work stoppages and other protests by his fellow prisoners. Despite this, officials noted him as "egocentric" and "antisocial," and the board consistently denied him parole.

Because of Jackson's indeterminate sentence, and the fact he was at the mercy of assessments and recommendations by guards, they – the guards – essentially determined whether or not he would ever be released from prison. And in the 1960s, when racism was prevalent, given that the majority of guards were white, things were not in Jackson's favor. Jackson argued that, no matter what he did, guards perceived his behavior as "revolutionary," which meant to prison officials he was rebellious and contemptuous toward authority. Whatever he did, or didn't do, seemed to work against him. For example, him not participating in work stoppages was, according to guards, because he was strategically concealing his leadership of those very strikes. He was powerless to dispute the guards' assessments, and because he pled guilty to the original robbery charge, he didn't have a right to an attorney during his board hearings, nor was he eligible to appeal the original case. Eventually, Jackson's hope began to vanish. As evident by the things he wrote about in his letters, he began to feel helpless and frustrated. He referred to prison guards as "pigs," expressed his sentence was unjust, and that he was being oppressed. He began to proudly proclaim himself a revolutionary and often talked about escaping.

$$$$$

The 1960s was an extremely political time in America, full of civil rights and social justice movements. This wasn't only the case on the outside, but in prison, too. Activism and revolutions took place. Prisoners began to protest, organize, and demand certain rights. They wanted to be heard in the courts. They wanted freedom of speech and association, and overall better treatment. Much of the organizing among prisoners took place along racial lines, and if not in practice, certainly in the eyes of prison officials, the line between being a racially-based political movement or a race-based prison gang became blurred. According to Carl Larson, who worked as a prison guard during this period and later a warden, the civil rights and social justice movements outside of prison aligned with the more divided and radical revolutionaries inside prison: "We had this 'revolution,' and it manifested itself with a lot of rhetoric – in colleges and jails. The manifestation in colleges was mainly peaceful – a lot of rhetoric and thought. In the prisons, it manifested in a lot of violence."

Jackson began studying radical political theorists like Karl Marx and Frantz Fanon around 1962, under the guidance of W.L. Nolen, another African-American prisoner who ran a reading group. Jackson would later say, "I met Marx, Lenin, Trotsky, Engels, and Mao when I entered prison and they redeemed me." Jackson and other revolutionaries like Eldridge Cleaver and Huey Newton, Black Panthers who were also incarcerated in California during the 1960s, encouraged black prisoners to become conscious of the racial discrimination going on inside the walls. They closely studied revolutionary theorists and promoted violent political activity. "The concept of nonviolence is a false ideal," Jackson wrote in one of these letters. And in another: "Politics is violence." Ultimately, the members of this reading group, including Jackson and Nolen, would create the Black Guerrilla Family (BGF), which was founded sometime around 1966, and they aligned themselves with the Black Panther Party. According to the BGF and its followers, it's a revolutionary political organization; according to prison officials, however, it's a black prison gang. "The Black Guerrilla Family and the Black Panthers, they had a political side... but they were mostly gangs, mafia," says Larson.

In January, 1967, Jackson appeared before the parole board and was denied again. "Of course, I could do the rest of my life in here," he told his family, referring to his indeterminate sentence.

In December of 1967 he again appeared before the board. At the previous hearing they'd promised him that, if he gave them 7-8 months clean, he'd be granted parole. When he reminded them of this, they said, "We never make deals like that." He was told he'd come back in a year.

In December of 1968, Jackson appeared before the board for the eighth time. After the hearing he was told by the institution employee who attended all his hearings that he'd been granted parole, and would be back on the streets March 4, 1969. He was excited and began telling everyone he had a "date," that he'd finally be going home. He even wrote his family and asked them to prepare. Three days later, however, he was told a mistake had been made, and consideration had been postponed for another six months. He was told he'd be transferred to Soledad State Prison (from San Quentin), and if he did well for six months, he'd be paroled for sure. He stayed out of trouble, but when the June 1969 hearing took place, he appeared before different board members. Of course, none of these board members could find any reference to the promise that had been made to him by the earlier board. He was denied another full year. Not surprisingly, Jackson's frustrations were at an all-time high. And what would happen next would prove to be the breaking point.

Murder Season

In January, 1970, tensions at Soledad State Prison were rising among black and white prisoners, and also black prisoners and white prison guards. Jackson was housed in "Y" wing, and his mentor, W.L. Nolen was in "O" wing, which had been locked down off and on for months. Recently, Nolen had circulated a petition among the prisoner population; he wanted to file a lawsuit against guards for harassment, abuse, and the endangerment of black prisoners. Prison officials were not happy about this, and it was causing even further tension between them and black prisoners, especially Nolen, the author of the complaint. Nolen anticipated some sort of retaliation by guards; however, he didn't know what would happen, or when.

On January 13, guards spontaneously released 15 prisoners from the locked-down "O" wing for yard. Seven were black, eight were white – each defined as racists by prison officials. Not surprisingly, a melee erupted. That's when Opie Miller, a white officer who was manning the gun tower, shot into the melee, killing three prisoners: Cleveland Edwards, Alvin Miller, and W.L. Nolen – all black. Nolen was shot right through his heart.

Soledad prisoners demanded murder charges be filed against officer Miller, but three days later, the District Attorney announced it was "justifiable homicide," and no charges would be filed. What seemed to be the targeting of W.L. and black prisoners raised questions about the motives of Miller, prison officials and the District Attorney. Later that night, John Vincent Mills, a white officer, was beat and thrown over the third tier, in "Y" wing. According to witnesses, there was an explosion of applause as the officer landed on the concrete floor, where he died. Prison authorities investigated the incident, and two weeks later charged those they claimed responsible: John Clutchette, Fleeta Drumgo, and George Jackson.

By this time, Jackson was 28 years old. His one-year-to-life sentence looked like it was going to become a death sentence. The same DA who announced he would not be filing charges against the white officer who killed three black prisoners, announced he would be seeking the death penalty for the three black prisoners accused of killing the one white cop.

Jackson was transferred back to San Quentin and held in the Adjustment Center. The Adjustment Center, or "AC" as it's often referred to, opened in 1960. It's a 3-story-high building, and at the time was considered a state-of-the-art lockdown facility. Prisoners were locked down for 23 hours a day and had no other human contact other than shouting out the bars to the other 27 prisoners on the tier. When a prisoner would leave their cell, they would do so in shackles, and when they returned – escorted both ways – they would be strip-searched to ensure they weren't smuggling anything back. Despite Jackson's almost complete isolation, however, violence continued.

On February 25, 1970, Fred Billings, a black prisoner who was housed near Jackson in the AC, died suspiciously in his cell. Prison officials said he started his cell on fire and choked to death. Prisoner witnesses, however, says he was beaten by guards and tear-gassed to death. In any case, black prisoners saw this as another attack by prison guards.

In March, the very month after the suspicious death of Billings, a white guard at San Quentin was stabbed. He survived, but James McClain, a black prisoner, was charged with the stabbing.

Three months after that, in June, Jackson was scheduled to appear before the parole board, but refused to go. By now, he saw no point.

On June 28, Jackson wrote a letter to Joan, a friend and member of the Soledad defense team (who happened to be white) stating, "I'm thinking of Jon now." Jon was Jackson's 17-year-old brother. "I wish there was a way to talk to him in private. They ran him off, too." Jackson was referring to Joan and Jon being denied visitation with him. "They certainly must be sure of themselves, I mean sure of being able to convict and hold and get rid of me, because they're not very concerned with making me mad. And they know I'll never forget."

In July, William Schull, a white officer was killed while on duty at Soledad. Seven black prisoners were charged with the murder. And on July 28, Joan and Jon visited with Jackson.

On August 7, just a little over a week after Joan and Jon's visit with Jackson, guards transported James McClain from San Quentin to the Marin County courthouse for the first day of his trial for stabbing the white guard. He was the first of black prisoners to stand trial on the attacks of white officers. By this time, McCain, along with the Soledad Brothers, had gained national support, thanks to Angela Davis, an assistant professor at the University of California, Los Angeles, and Jackson's younger brother Jonathan, who had built the support by claiming the Soledad Brothers' innocence and bringing publicity to the case.

The trial began and the first witness took that stand. Then, out of nowhere, Jon Jackson burst into the courtroom with a pistol and a carbine rifle. With the help of McClain and two other prisoners, William Christmas and Ruchell Magee, who were there to testify for McClain, Jon took the judge, Harold Haley, District Attorney Gary Thomas, and three jurors hostage, demanding release of the Soledad Brothers. They put the hostages into a rented van, and according to eyewitnesses, fastened a shotgun to the judge's neck with adhesive tape and some sort of strap, so it pointed directly under the judge's chin. By now, the Marin County police arrived and joined forces with San Quentin guards, and when the van began to pull out of the courthouse parking lot, they unloaded a flurry of bullets into it, killing Jackson, McClain, and Christmas. The judge was also killed, though it's unclear if it was from police fire or the shotgun taped under his chin. The DA was permanently paralyzed. Ruchell Magee and the jurors survived and the event made national headlines.

As of August 7, the total amount of deaths both inside and outside of prison: 10.

The guns used by Jon were eventually traced to Angela Davis, who'd purchased them legally over the previous two years. She became a fugitive until

October when she was caught and put in jail. (She eventually stood trial in 1972 for the kidnapping and murder of the judge, but was acquitted by an all-white jury.)

George Jackson remained in San Quentin's Adjustment Center while awaiting trial for the murder of officer Mills. In the fall of 1970, he released his first book, *Soledad Brother*, which he dedicated to his brother Jonathan. The book is a collection of letters he'd written to his mother, father, siblings and lawyers between the years of 1964 and 1970. *Soledad Brothers* received critical acclaim and was compared to books like *Autobiography of Malcolm X* and *Soul on Ice*, written by Black Panther and prisoner Eldridge Cleaver. The final letter in *Soledad Brother* is addressed to Joan and dated August 9, 1970 – two days after Jon was killed by police. It reads in part: "I want people to wonder at what forces created him, terrible, vindictive, cold, calm man-child, courage in one hand, the machine gun in the other, scourge of the unrighteous – an ox for the people to ride!!!... I can't go any further, it would just be a love story about the baddest brother this world has ever had the privilege to meet, and it's just not popular or safe – to say I love him."

By 1971, Jackson's legal team was hard at work in preparation of his upcoming murder trial which was set to begin August 24. In April, Jackson's legal team filed a complaint that prison officials were interfering with his defense by hiding and paroling witnesses favorable to him, and threatening others into testifying against him. Several prisoners wrote declarations confirming these claims.

By August, one year had passed since Jon was killed, and Jackson completed a second book of letters and essays titled *Blood in My Eye*. (This book would not be published until the following year.) He also had a substantial legal team and was nationally known as one of the Soledad Brothers.

On August 18, Jackson rewrote his will, leaving all royalties and control of his legal defense fund to the Black Panther Party.

What happened next, however, remains somewhat of a mystery, even to this day, full of contradictions, controversy and conspiracy theories, but it goes something like this...

The Dragon Has Come

On Saturday, August 21, at around 2pm, attorney Stephen Bingham arrived at San Quentin for a scheduled visit with Jackson. Bingham, who came from a wealthy family in Connecticut, was exactly the same age as Jackson: 29. He was a graduate of Boalt Hall Law School at the University of California, Berkeley. Along with Bingham was Vanita Anderson, an "investigator" for the defense team. She brought with her a tape recorder, and Bingham had with him a bunch of legal papers, as well as the galleys (typeset pages) of Jackson's new book. Both Bingham and Anderson consented to a search of their persons and items, and according to a *Washington Post* article that would be published a few days later, Bingham passed through a metal detector and a guard inspected the tape recorder's battery case.

Anderson was ultimately denied entry because she had already visited Jackson earlier that week, and a day prior to this (on August 20), James Park, the Associate Warden (AW) at San Quentin during this time, issued a new policy limiting "reporter" interviews of prisoners in "lockups," like the AC, to once every 90 days, due to the enormous amount of attention "famous" prisoners like Jackson were getting. Whether Anderson was an investigator for the defense team or a reporter is unclear. In any case, Bingham was Jackson's lawyer, so his visit could not be denied and he was allowed entry.

According to Bingham, after the guard on duty searched the tape recorder and determined nothing was in it, he encouraged Bingham to take it into the prison since Anderson was denied entry. But Carl Larson, who at the time was working as a correctional counselor at Chino State Prison and recalls discussing the day's events with AW Park, says, "When Bingham came into the prison, he had a tape recorder, he was going to visit with George Jackson, and the officer at the gate wanted to take the tape recorder apart. The lawyer argued, got offended, resisted, asked for a supervisor. The officer calls a lieutenant, says, 'You can't come in with that.' The officer calls Jim Park, and Jim Park approved it, said, 'Let it go in.'"

Once Bingham was allowed into the prison, guards escorted Jackson to the room where his visit with Bingham was to take place. Jackson sat across from Bingham at a wooden table that had no barriers, and guards intermittently checked on the two. The meeting only lasted about 15 minutes, then Bingham left with tape recorder and papers in hand.

Around 2:25 pm, officer Frank DeLeon escorted Jackson back to the AC, where officer Urbano Rubiaco began to strip-search Jackson before letting him back to his cell. Reportedly, Rubiaco asked Jackson about what appeared to be a pencil or something in his hair, and that's when Jackson pulled out a gun, inserted a clip and pointed it at officers. He then shouted, "This is it!" and ordered officer Rubiaco to open all of the prisoners' cells, where he and other black prisoners took hostage all four guards (officers Frank DeLeon, Paul Krasnes, Kenneth McCray, and Charles Breckenridge), and two white prisoners (John Lynn and Ronald Kane). Sometime while this was going on, sergeant Jere Graham arrived at the AC to assist officer DeLeon on another escort, unaware of what was taking place, and when he arrived, he, too, was taken hostage. Jackson reportedly yelled, "The dragon has come!" – a reference to a poem written by North Vietnamese leader Ho Chi Minh about the power of imprisonment to generate a revolution.

During the revolt, according to the *San Francisco Chronicle*, officer Breckenridge had his throat slashed and was dragged to Jackson's cell. He survived, but officers DeLeon and Krasnes, along with Lynn and Kane, the two white inmates, were killed, and their bodies thrown on top of Breckenridge. Sergeant Graham was also killed, though it's unclear where his body was left.

When prison officials who were not in the Adjustment Center became aware of what was going on, they alerted the California Highway Patrol and Marin County Sheriff who came heavily armed and blocked all access roads to the prison, demanding prisoners give up. Jackson reportedly yelled to his fellow participants, "It's me they want!," so with gun in hand, along with Johnny Spain, another black prisoner, he ran out of the AC, where he was immediately gunned down by a marksman; Spain ducked for cover under a bush. There are conflicting stories about how many shots Jackson suffered, and exactly where he was shot. Most say Jackson was shot in the back and the bullet ricocheted off his spine and came out his head. Others say the bullet traveled the other way. Soledad Brother John Clutchette says Jackson was shot in the back by the guard in the gun tower, then when guards gathered around him, they shot him again, in the head. However Jackson was shot, he died quickly.

When guards finally entered the AC, they found a bloodbath where the revolt had taken place. Three guards and two prisoners, all who were white, had been shot and/or stabbed to death. Breckenridge, of course, had his throat slashed, but survived. Messages were found in Jackson's cell that said, "Take the bullets out the bag," and "Hurry and give me the piece in the bag. Keep the bullets."

According to historian Dan Berger, the guards then retaliated by stripping, handcuffing, and hog-tying the remaining 26 prisoners in AC, and left them naked in the San Quentin yard next to where Jackson laid dead. During the following days they were repeatedly interrogated and beaten. Warden Louis S. Nelson reportedly told them, "None of you will ever leave here alive."

$$$$$

What exactly happened on August 21, 1971, we may never know. California correctional authorities have their version, prisoners and Jackson supporters have theirs, and journalists and investigators have theirs, which usually lies somewhere in the middle. Prison officials will usually tell of Jackson's attempt to escape, claiming his lawyer, Bingham, smuggled him in a gun and an afro wig to hide it under, inside the tape recorder. Some Jackson supporters claim he was not trying to escape, but instead was set up for assassination by the Criminal Conspiracy Section of the Los Angeles Police Department, who had infiltrated the Black Panthers in Los Angeles and the Bay Area in an attempt to track and control the revolutionaries. Others say Jackson was set up as an escape attempt so "they" could kill him for the murder of officer Mills, and because of the power and influence he'd gained over other black prisoners, who'd been assaulting and killing white prison guards.

There's credibility to the theory Jackson was attempting to escape. After all, he openly spoke about doing so. Then again, with close enough examination of all the evidence, the other theories are possible as well. Regardless of what happened, however, the stories by prison officials are plagued with inconsistencies – including what should be hard facts, which is particularly troubling. For example, the type of gun Jackson was said to have had often changed. Some said it was a .25, others said a .38, and others said a 9mm Astra M-600 semiautomatic pistol. How can this not be clear? The 9mm Astra seems to be what most have settled on, but what's strange about this is that a 9mm Astra M-600 is 9 inches long, weighs over two pounds and is nicknamed "The Pipe wrench"; something probably impossible to conceal under an afro wig, or inside a tape recorder. (Many say it most certainly would not have fit.) Daniel P. Scarborough, the officer who was responsible for processing Bingham, later tried to clarify what happened by saying Bingham concealed the gun between stapled pieces of paper. I guess only Bingham truly knows whether or not he smuggled the gun and afro wig into Jackson that day, and if he did, how he did it. Immediately after the incident, he went on the run, fleeing the country for 13 years. He returned in 1984, however, to stand trial, argued guards had brought Jackson the gun, hoping he'd be killed. Bingham was acquitted of all charges relating to the August 21, 1971 event in 1986. (There are theories that the gun had been smuggled into Jackson in pieces, over time, where he was able to put it together himself. Could the "pencil" officer Rubiaco thought he saw in Jackson's hair have been a barrel? The notes later found in Jackson's cell lend some credibility to the theory Jackson had the gun, or at least some of it, before August 21.)

Six prisoners were ultimately charged in the events that took place in the Adjustment Center: Fleeta Drumgo, one of the original Soledad Brothers; Luis Talamantez; Willie Tate; David Johnson; Johnny Spain; and Hugo "Yogi" Pinell. Drumgo was acquitted of all charges and paroled shortly after. However, he was shot to death in 1979, in Oakland, under mysterious circumstances. There were reportedly two shooters, neither of whom have been caught. Talamantez and Tate were acquitted on all charges and paroled sometime in the 1970s. Johnson was convicted on one count of assault for strangling officer Breckenridge, but was also paroled sometime in the 70s. Spain was convicted on two counts of murder for killing officers DeLeon and Graham, but the conviction was overturned in 1982, and he paroled in 1988. Pinell was convicted on two counts of assault for slashing the throats of officers Breckenridge and Rubiaco, both of whom survived, and remained in solitary confinement until he was murdered under controversial circumstances in 2015. These men became known as the "San Quentin Six," and the trial, which cost over 2 million dollars and lasted over 16 months, was dubbed "The Longest Trial" by *Time* magazine. It took the jury 124 days to deliberate, and when the verdicts came in, it took Judge Henry J. Broderick 24 minutes to read them.

Jackson's legacy lives on today through prison lore, not only in California, but across America. Prisoners, especially black, tend to view him as an inspiration: a man who, come what may, stood up for

MIKE ENEMIGO

his people against a racist, oppressive, and abusive systems. To them he is a martyr. To prison officials, however, he is the most dangerous prisoner ever housed in California – a terrorist. Jackson was "a sociopath, a very personable hoodlum" who "didn't give a shit about the revolution," says San Quentin's Associate Warden James Park. Today, even the slightest association with Jackson can lead to discipline for prisoners, such as being validated as a member of the Black Guerrilla Family, or in the case of Stanley "Tookie" Williams, being used to justify an execution. (Williams, co-founder of the Crips who turned outspoken advocate for nonviolence, and who had been on San Quentin's death row since 1981, sought clemency from Governor Arnold Schwarzenegger in 2005. Governor Schwarzenegger denied the petition, however, at least partly because Williams included Jackson in the dedication of one of his books. Williams was executed on December 14, 2005.) But not only in prison does Jackson's legacy live on. In 2003, rapper Ja Rule titled his album *Blood in My Eye* in homage of Jackson and his bestselling book. Even Bob Dylan released a single in which he titled *George Jackson*, and several other musicians have paid homage as well.

In 2007, the movie *Black August*, which recaptured the last 14 months of Jackson's life was released. Jackson has also been acclaimed throughout the world as one of the most powerful and eloquent black writers.

To this day, over 50 years later, on the path to the prison yard at San Quentin, an American flag perpetually flies at half-staff to commemorate August 21, 1971, the deadliest day in California prison history.

FLY BALL

I once had a celly named Ronnie. He was an older guy who lived on the bottom tier, the tier I wanted to be on, and one day his celly moved out, so I moved in. I didn't really know Ronnie too well before this, but he seemed decent. He was a porter, so he was hardly ever in the cell anyway. And when he was, we got along well; we'd chat and he'd tell me a lot of stories about 'back in the day,' etc.

Ronnie really liked to gamble, and I really like to make money. So, since Ronnie was pretty good at gambling and I had a bunch of extra cosmetics and shit (prison money) sitting in paper bags under the bottom bunk, I'd let Ronnie gamble with my money. In exchange, when he won, we'd split the winnings. Sure, it was a no-lose situation for him, since he got to gamble with my money, but I didn't really care.

I always had a lot of shit coming from canteen and packages. Ronnie didn't really have shit other than what he'd hustle from the gambling table, most of which would go right back in the pot. So, since he was my celly and I thought we were cool, I'd give him soups, bags of chips, boxes of Nutty Bars, etc. This is on top of giving him money to gamble with.

Ronnie was a dope fiend. He loved heroin. I don't like living with guys who use like he did, but I had a little respect for him because he'd never actually cluck his shit for dope. He was kind of a "responsible" dope fiend; he'd only use when he'd hustle up money to but it, or someone would kick him down something for free. Anyway, one time Ronnie slammed some heroin and overdosed. He fell flat on the floor, needle and everything. I immediately sat him up and started pouring cold water (from the toilet) over him; his head, nuts, etc. I also slapped him across his face a few time as hard as I could, which, I admit, I kinda liked because he had been getting on my nerves anyway. I thought the dude was going to die, but after 5-6 minutes he came to. Long story short; I gave him money to gamble with, food to eat, and I saved his life, ya dig?

During this time, I had a pen pal from Texas named Rose. She was a good-looking lady, a few years older than me and already settled down in life. Rose was very supportive and was going to help me with some online aspects of my business. She was a very valuable friend with only one requirement; that I never, *ever* give her address out to anyone. I assured her I never would, and I meant it.

After living with Ronnie for a couple months, I moved into another block to be with some of my folks. A few months after that, I was sent to the hole for some bullshit. During this entire time, Rose was riding strong.

I'd been in the hole for about five months when in comes Ronnie. Since I was cool with him and I was already established, I sent him a bunch of food, cosmetics, magazines, etc.

It was about a month after Ronnie arrived that I

received a letter from Rose telling me how I'd betrayed her, and that I'd never hear from her again because I did the one thing to her I swore I'd never do; I gave her address out, to some schmuck named Ronnie.

I wrote Rose back and tried to explain that I never gave her address to anyone. I explained that Ronnie was an old celly who had must've written her address down while we were cellies, or the cops gave him one of my letter after I moved out. I promised her I'm much too selfish to ever want to share her with anyone. However, to this day, I've never heard from her again.

Although aware that Ronnie had betrayed me in one of the worst possible ways of betraying someone in prison, I didn't let him know that I knew. Instead, when I'd be escorted past his cell on my way to the yard, I'd smile, tell him what's up, and ask him if he needed anything. I didn't want him to know I knew what he'd done because I knew I'd see him again someday.

A year later, back in general population at another prison, me and about five others were called out of our building to go pick up our quarterly packages. At the time we were called out, there was nobody on the yard; just us.

While waiting for the package officer to call my name, a line of about eight new arrivals were escorted from the orientation building to the laundry room to get their state-issued clothing. Among the new arrivals? Ronnie. I cannot explain to you how happy I was to see him....

Being that I was about to get my package, it obviously was not a good time to confront Ronnie. So, I pulled my hat down low, turned my back to the group he was in so he wouldn't notice me, and smiled. A few minutes later, he was escorted back to the orientation building. A few minutes after that I was issued my package and then went back to my own building.

When program opened up later that day, the first thing I did was go talk to a guy on the yard named Jay that knew both Ronnie and I and told him that Ronnie had just rolled up. I told Jay that Ronnie had not seen me, and if he asked about me at all, to say he hadn't seen me on that yard and didn't think I was there. I told Jay to even tell Ronnie that he – Jay – had a problem with me, and when he saw me he was going to fuck me up. I wanted Ronnie to really believe that Jay hadn't seen me, and also feel that he had an ally. This way, he would never see me coming.

Ronnie ended up being on a different tier than me so I never went to the yard at the same time he did. Days, weeks, and then months had went by and I still had yet to see him.

Then, one day, while on the yard, Jay had come up to me and let me know that Ronnie had just went into the nurse's office, and would be coming out soon. I told him to go wait for Ronnie to come out, and when he did, to convince him to walk the long way back, all the way around the track. In case Ronnie didn't go along with Jay, I went and sat down on the ground, in front of Ronnie's building, on the other side of a table where I could see him when he came out, but he couldn't see me. If necessary, I would just intercept him before he made it to his building.

I sat there for about ten minutes, and then out came Ronnie. I saw Jay immediately walk up to him and start conversing. Instead of walking toward me, they started walking the other way – the long way. The plan was going nicely.

Once they started walking away, I got up, pulled my hat low and followed. My plan was to wait for them to get as far away from the main tower as possible, so I can make my move and at least try to get away with it. Once they were about there, I sped up to a speed that would allow me to catch up with them as soon as they were exactly where I wanted to meet up with them at. My timing was perfect.

As soon as we all arrived to the spot where I'd make my move, Jay turned around to see what was going on; I was right behind him. When he saw me, he made a little space between himself and Ronnie so I could slide right in and do my thing.

Without Ronnie even realizing it, I'd stepped right in the middle of him and Jay; Ronnie was to my left. Ronnie was talking, and when he looked up and to his right, he no longer saw Jay, he saw me. At the exact time he saw me, I said, "Hey, Ronnie; how you doin'?" and immediately crushed my fist into his mouth, causing him to drop like the sack of shit he is. While he was on the ground, I kicked him in the face and stomped on his head; and for good measure, I stomped on his glasses, too, crushing them into pieces. While Ronnie was splitting up teeth and blood, I said to him, "If you ever steal from me again, I'll fuckin' whack you."

I was about to jump back on top of him when I suddenly noticed that no alarm had went off. That meant that I had gotten away with what I'd done so far, and I decided I was content with that. I started walking away, but had I heard the alarm go off, my plan was to run back over there and smash him until the officers came. If I was caught; might as well get all the money, right?

For a while Ronnie had sat at the table near where everything had happened, trying to gain his senses. Then he went back to the nurse, and a few minutes after that he was escorted to the prison's main hospital to get himself put back together. I could've sworn he was going to tell on me, but he didn't. Turns out he said he got hit by a softball – a softball game was going on and occasionally prisoners do get hit by a fly ball zipping through the air.

A few weeks later I got word the Ronnie had rolled it up off the yard. He told the guards his life was in danger. I'm not quite sure if he really felt that way, or was just embarrassed for getting it the way he did. Whatever his reason(s), I haven't seen him again, which obviously is something I'm OK with. I did what I had to do and that's that.

There are two morals to this story: 1) There are scumbags who will steal your addresses and write your people when they think they can get away with it. 2) Karma's a bitch; people who do this will eventually get hit by a softball zipping through the air.

JOE

Joe Morgan was born April 10, 1929, to Croatian immigrants in San Pedro, California. Shortly after, he and his mother moved to the Maravilla Projects in East Los Angeles, and in the late 1930s he joined Ford Maravilla – a Chicano (Mexican American) street gang, and one of the oldest documented gangs in Los Angeles.

When Morgan was 16, he became romantically involved with a 32-year-old woman. Even at a young age he had a thirst for blood, and he demonstrated this when he beat the woman's husband to death with a tire iron and buried him in a shallow grave in the Malibu hills. He was eventually caught, and although a minor, he was held at the Los Angeles County Jail. While awaiting trial, however, the criminally crafty Morgan posed as his cellmate, who was awaiting transfer to a juvenile facility, and escaped. He was recaptured shortly after, convicted of second-degree murder and sent to San Quentin State Prison, where he served 9 years.

Morgan paroled in 1955, but just a year later he robbed a West Covina bank using a machine gun. He made off with $17,000, but was ultimately caught and sent back to prison. According to Mexican-Mafia-member-turned-FBI-snitch, Rene "Boxer" Enriquez, Morgan was shot in the leg during the robbery, which caused him to lose his leg. (William Dunn, police officer and writer, says Morgan was shot in the leg while hiding from law enforcement for murder.) Prison officials began referring to Morgan as "Pegleg," though nobody called him this to his face, and he certainly didn't let something as "minor" as the loss of a leg slow him down: "He was the one-legged man that you hear about in the ass-kicking contest," says Richard Valdemar, a retired 33-year Los Angeles Sheriff's Department veteran gang investigator. "He was a champion on the prison handball courts. He was physically fit and very able to move around and fight."

In 1957, at Dual Vocational Institution (DVI), a California Youth Authority that is now an adult prison in Tracy, California, a group of young Chicano street-gang members came together to create The Mexican Mafia, or "La Eme" as it's often called – a gang of gangs – as a way to protect themselves from prison predators and other gangs, such as the Blue Birds – the original members of the Aryan Brotherhood (AB). By 1961, however, according to famed crime reporter Chris Blatchford, administrators at DVI, alarmed by the escalating violence committed by The Mexican Mafia, transferred a number of the young Eme members to San Quentin State Prison in hopes of discouraging their behavior by intermingling them with the older, more seasoned convicts. However, it backfired. According to legend, Rodolpho "Cheyenne" Cadena, one of the young Eme members transferred to San Quentin, who was already in prison for stabbing someone to death, was met be a six-foot-five, 300-

pound black prisoner who kissed him on the face and declared that the scrawny 18-year-old would be his "bitch." A short time later, Cheyenne returned with a shank (a prison-made knife), walked up to the unsuspecting predator, and brutally stabbed him to death in front of more than a thousand inmates on the yard, all of who refused to step forward as witnesses. This not only got the Mafia an enormous amount of respect on the yard, it solidified the wise-beyond-his-years Cheyenne as a fearless leader of the gang.

Also in 1961, Morgan was transferred from Folsom State Prison to the Los Angeles County Jail so he could testify on behalf of another prisoner. However, this was just a guise so the criminal mastermind could escape. He ended up leading eleven other inmates through a pipe shaft, reportedly using hacksaw blades he hid in his prosthesis. The escape was the largest break in Los Angeles County Jail history and featured on the front page of *The L.A. Times*. Morgan was caught a week later, however, while shopping for groceries, but not without bolstering his legend as a certified criminal mastermind.

Upon Morgan's recapture, he was sent to San Quentin. Already from a Varrio (Chicano street gang) and running with Chicanos, Morgan began running with members of La Eme, becoming best friends with their leader, Cheyenne. With Cheyenne's reputation built on blood, and Morgan's also built on blood (having already done time for murder and suspected of having committed others), along with jail breaks, their friendship seemed a perfect match. Morgan, 14 years older and a more experienced criminal than Cheyenne, became his criminal mentor. Morgan helped him build upon the newly-formed Mafia. Because of this, many claimed Morgan as one of the founders of La Eme, but others say he wasn't one of the founders, though he was a major part of its architecture and organizing.

"Joe wasn't an official member until 1972, after Cheyenne was killed. Don't get me wrong, he was one of the fellas and highly respected, but he wasn't officially brought in until after Cheyenne was killed, because originally you had to be of Mexican decent to a member," says Danny "Pache" Nava, a former member of La Eme who was brought in in 1977 by first-generation member Abraham Hernandez and Robert "Robot" Salas. "After Cheyenne was killed, though, they wanted Joe to officially take the chair since he had the majority of connections anyway, and that's when he was formally inducted." "As far as we were concerned, he was Mexican," says former Mexican Mafia hitman Ramon "Mundo" Mendoza. "If anybody ever called him a 'white boy,' I have no doubt he would have killed them. He knew what he was as far as his genes were concerned. But his heart was Chicano." Morgan spoke fluent Spanish, studied Mexican and Aztec history, and taught himself how to speak Nahuatl, an ancient Aztec dialect.

Morgan, known for his skin-shaved head, wooden leg, dark piercing eyes and appetite for blood, led the Mafia along with Cheyenne to prominence in the California prison system by terrorizing unorganized ethnic groups, primarily other Mexicans and Chicanos, and gaining control over things such as drug sales, porn, extortion, prostitution and even murder for hire.

As the Mafia's power increased, the gang spread like wildfire throughout California prisons. They became a major power player in the proverbial "game" of prison. Eventually, however, like oftentimes when people acquire an enormous amount of power, an abuse of such power can follow, and Chicano prisoners who were not affiliated, and therefore open to prey by The Mexican Mafia, became fed-up with members of La Eme bullying them, stealing their valuables, and sometimes even stabbing and killing them. As a result, in the mid-60s, a group of them in Soledad State Prison secretly came together to form their own gang, which they called "Nuestra Familia," — Spanish for "Our Family." Many of the early members of Nuestra Familia (NF) were from southern California, but they soon began to attract Chicanos from northern California, who the Mafia treated as inferior, claiming them to be just a bunch of "farmeros" — farmers. Tension arose, eventually boiling over in 1968 when

Robert "Robot" Salas, an Eme member from East L.A., "stole" a pair of shoes from a "northern" Chicano. This kicked off a riot in which 19 prisoners were stabbed and one Eme associate murdered, and from this point on, the NF was established as a major rival of The Mexican Mafia.

Morgan continued to expand La Eme, creating alliances with other crime syndicates like the Aryan Brotherhood, Mexican drug cartel members who were incarcerated in California, and even the Italian Mafia that was operating in Los Angeles. He was extremely business savvy and charismatic. "His ability to forge relationships with the Italian Mafia, the Aryan Brotherhood and Mexican drug cartels was due to his people skills," says Rodrigo Ribera D'Ebre, author of *Urban Politics: The Political Culture of Sur 13 Gangs*. "Joe Morgan was known to be a leader."

"With his savvy, his manipulative skills, his intelligence, his charisma and his knack for being profitable, he could easily have been the president of a major corporation," says Mendoza. But while there was a side to Morgan that was humane and personable, Mendoza says "Part of him was cruel and coldblooded."

"Joe Morgan had two personalities," says Valdemar. "One level-headed and diplomatic who intended to do business the right way, but if you crossed The Mexican Mafia, he'd be the first to go to war. He did his share of killing. When he killed he became a different person. He was very, very violent when he wanted to be and participated in plenty of stabbings. It's not like he was the financial arm, or the diplomatic arm, he was just a good soldier for The Mexican Mafia. Just as violent as any of the other gang members."

When Morgan got out of prison in the late 60s, early 70s, he did so with the objective of taking the gang to new heights. He didn't only want to control prison, he wanted to control all of Los Angeles, starting with East L.A. He began taxing Chicano street gangs. If they wanted to sell dope, they had to buy it from La Eme; if they wanted to engage in other profitable crimes, they'd have to kick a portion of the profits to the Mafia. Failure to do so and they'd face the gang's wrath when they went to prison – where they'd surely end up eventually. Morgan sent this message clearly: "Buy our dope and pay us a tax or die," explains Valdemar. "You hear about the Italian mob sometimes breaking your leg or intimidating you or threatening you, but The Mexican Mafia guys just kill you. There were all these deaths that were occurring on the streets in the 70s and that was The Mexican Mafia taking over the drug industry in East L.A. and the surrounding areas." Morgan used the underworld network he built to further the Mafia's agenda: He outsourced Mafia murders to the bloodthirsty Aryan Brotherhood; he used his Mexican drug cartel contacts to smuggle kilos of heroin and cocaine into Los Angeles; and he collaborated with the Italians on white-collar crimes, and by supplying them with drugs from his Mexican contacts.

In 1971, Morgan committed the first prison-gang street execution in Los Angeles when Eme member

Alphonso "Pachie" Alvarez began collecting taxes from street gangs without kicking up a share of the profits to Mafia members behind bars. Morgan shot him twice in the head; his body was later found in a secluded area in Monterey Park.

Meanwhile, in prison, Cheyenne, who was active in Latino political organizations like the Brown Berets, had a vision of statewide dominance, both in prison and out, and wanted to unite La Eme with the Nuestra Familia. This was reportedly looked down upon by Morgan and other members of the Mafia, and this is where a couple conspiracy theories take place. In December of 1972, Cheyenne arranged to be transferred to Chino State Prison for a peace discussion with NF member Death Row Joe Gonzalez. Reportedly, in an effort to sabotage the mission, Eme leaders had two NF members killed, essentially ending any possibility of peace. In response to the two NF members being killed, on December 17, the NF stabbed Cheyenne over 50 times, beat him with a pipe, threw him over the third tier onto the concrete floor, then ran down and stabbed him several more times. One theory is that the Eme only wanted to sabotage the peace talk, unaware that Cheyenne would still be put in a position to be harmed. Another theory is that the Eme had turned their back on Cheyenne and knew they were putting him position to be killed. Those who believe La Eme had not turned their backs on Cheyenne, however, point out that as a result of his murder, La Eme put a "kill on sight" order on all members of the NF, and in just the first year after the murder, 31 prisoners were killed in a tit-for-tat war.

What actually happened regarding the murder of Cheyenne, we may never truly know. What we do know, however, is that Morgan became the official Godfather of The Mexican Mafia from this point forward, until he died.

In 1977, Morgan was convicted or trying to arrange the murder of a Seal Beach drug dealer for failing to pay the Mafia money. Unaware that Eme member Ramon "Mundo" Mendoza had turned on him, he asked Mendoza to commit the murder, supplying him with a picture of the intended target, a house key, and a .45 caliber pistol inside a brown paper bag. Mendoza testified against Morgan and Morgan received a life sentence.

In December of 1989, California opened the doors to the notorious Pelican Bay State Prison which contained a new, state-of-the-art lockdown "Security Housing Unit," or "SHU" (pronounced "shoe") as it's often called, where California would send its high-profile, prison gang members, including Morgan. Morgan continued to manage The Mexican Mafia from his prison cell in Pelican Bay, despite being locked down 23 hours a day and having virtually no physical contact with other humans.

In 1992, Morgan and other members of The Mexican Mafia, including Cheyenne, were cast into the public eye with the release of actor-and-producer Edward James Olmos's movie *American Me*, which was fictional, but based on actual events. Morgan and other members of the Mafia were outraged by the movie, especially by the portrayal of Cheyenne, who was called "Santana" in the movie, and played by Olmos himself. In the movie, Santana was sodomized by a white inmate, who he immediately retaliated against by killing (probably inspired by the story of Cheyenne being kissed by the black inmate who he later came back and stabbed to death), and also because, in the movie, Santana was killed by members of La Eme after falling out of favor with them (probably inspired by the theory Morgan and the Eme had set Cheyenne up to be murdered by the NF). In the movie, members of the Mafia killed Santana very similar to the way Cheyenne was killed by the Nuestra Familia in real life.

As a result of *American Me*, Morgan ordered the murders of three past and present Mafia members and associates who served as consultants for Olmos and movie producers.

Charles "Charlie Brown" Manriquez, a member of La Eme, was murdered in an L.A. housing project in March, 1992, less than two weeks after the film premiered. In May, Aria Lizarraga, known as "The

Gang Lady," who played a grandmother in the movie and used to run drugs for La Eme, was shot to death right in front of her own home. And a little over a year later, Eme member Manual "Rocky" Luna was murdered. Olmos received several death threats, and was so worried that he contacted the FBI and even went into hiding for a period of time.

Morgan filed a lawsuit against Olmos and movie producers for $500,000 for basing one of the characters ("JD," played by actor William Forsythe) on his life without his permission. It's been reported that Olmos offered Morgan's wife $5,000 as a settlement, but that she refused it. Olmos also reportedly requested to speak with Morgan, but Morgan refused to speak with him. The suit was ultimately dismissed, but it's said that Olmos had been "greenlighted," meaning placed on The Mexican Mafia's hit list. Some say, however, that Olmos ultimately paid the Mafia a large sum of money to remove the greenlight, arguing as proof that he is still alive today.

In 1993, Morgan became ill, and on October 4, he was transferred from Pelican Bay to the hospital ward in Corcoran State Prison, where, on October 27, he was diagnosed with inoperable liver cancer. Conspiracy theorists argue that Morgan was poisoned by prison authorities because he'd become too powerful. Morgan ultimately died on November 9, 1993, at the age of 64.

Morgan's legacy lives on today as "one of the best who's ever done it." "When you were in Joe's presence, you could feel it. You could tell he possessed not one false molecule," says Nava. "Joe even had politicians in pocket. We maintained it for as long as we could, and we did well, but things were never the same after Joe died," he adds.

Even Mendoza, the turncoat who put Morgan away for life was impacted by Morgan's death. "When I heard that Joe died, I felt a small twang of guilt," he says. "I didn't really want to give him up. He had an option of choosing a different path. But he made his commitment and he took it to the grave."

"He had his own sense of honor, whether you agreed with it or not, and he lived by it," says DEA agent Joe Moody, who headed the state prison gang task force in the mid-1970s. "It would be nothing you'd want to hand down to your children. But in his world, he walked above a lot of people."

MURDER SEASON

On August 27, 2020, Juan M. Boyzo became the sixth prisoner in nine months to die at the hands of fellow inmates using homemade weapons at High Desert State Prison in Susanville, California. The first, Edgardo Herrera, was killed by Roger Vasquez and Douglas Leon on November 27, 2019. All three men had previously received additional sentences for possessing weapons or controlled substances in the prison, and Vasquez had also been given an additional term for assaulting another prisoner.

In January 2020, two more prisoners were stabbed to death by fellow inmates: Richard Leyva, 37, who died on January 7 at the hands of Luis Ortega, 36, and Vincent Martinez, 37, and Richard Prieto, 44, who was killed by Jose R. Zapien, 31, on January 28. Leyva had also received extra time for an earlier assault on another prisoner, while Castillo had been given an additional sentence for possessing a weapon in the prison.

On May 1, 2020, Michael M. Ramadanovic, 65, was fatally stabbed by fellow prisoners Rodney Rice and Robert Smith, both 28. Smith and the victim had each been sentenced to extra time for assaulting fellow prisoners.

Boyzo, 25, was stabbed to death by Joseph M. Gama, 22, and Joseph B. Sua, 29, who is serving an extended sentence for possessing a controlled substance in prison. The 25-year-old maximum-security facility in Lassen County employees about 1,200. As of April 2020, it held 3,286 prisoners, more than 141 percent of its design capacity of 2,334. It is located in Lassen County, along with the minimum-security Federal Correctional Institution at Herlong. Together the three hold 9,414 prisoners in a county with a population of just 30,573.

Meanwhile, life goes on for the rest of us....

SMILEY

There was a time when I was having cash smuggled in. In prison, cash is usually worth double with the dope-man. So, what I'd do is have a bunch of $20.00 bills smuggled in, and I'd give each $20.00 bill to a guy named Old Man Smiley in exchange for $30.00 worth of canteen. I didn't care about any dope, nor did I want to do any hustling, so $30.00 worth of canteen in exchange for $20.00 cash was a come-up for me.

Old Man Smiley, on the other hand, did like to use dope, and he didn't mind working twists and busting little moves to get it. So, I'd give him the cash, and what he'd do is take the $20.00 bill to the dope-man, get a small $50.00 paper or a fat $40.00 paper, cut

$10.00-$20.00 worth off of it for himself, sell $30.00 worth for canteen, then pay me with that – the canteen.

I did this with Old Man Smiley a lot, and he's the only one I did it with because I'm very private when it comes to my business (legal or illegal), and I didn't want anyone else to know what I was doing. Besides, our system was smooth and it allowed us both to win.

One day, out of the blue, some dope fiend named Ruben sent me a little kite that said: "Would you like to trade any of that for the opposite?" Now, I knew who Ruben was, but I didn't actually know him. I'd never dealt with the guy before because he comes off as a fuckin' weasel, and I wasn't interested in ever dealing with him because, well, he comes off as a fuckin' weasel. Besides, what the fuck is "the opposite"? So, I threw the kite in the toilet, flushed it and went about my business.

Later that day, when Ruben was let out of his cell for program, he came up to my cell and asked me if I needed anything. Now, remember, I don't even know or talk to this guy, and all of a sudden he's concerned with what I may or may not need? I threw the up the Playboy bunny to the guy and told him I was straight in hopes he'd get the fuck away from my cell. However, then the schmuck put his face in the side crack of my door, and with his stale-ass coffee breath said, "Did you get my kite?" I'd forgotten all about getting the kite until he'd mentioned it, but once reminded of it I told him I had: "Yeah, I got it. I don't know what the fuck you're talking about." He said: "Bro, I want some of that black. I have some white right now; would you like to trade some?" I said, "Black? I ain't got nothin' like that," He said, "Come on, bro; I'm cool. I just want to know if we can trade a little, ya know?" I said, "I ain't got nothin' like that, Playboy. Sorry." He looked at me with a look that's supposed to tell me he ain't stupid, and that he's offended I was lying to him. Then the weasel walked away.

For the next few days, I noticed that this Ruben guy would make himself known in my presence; you know, work out by me on the yard, sit by me at chow, etc. It was very obvious to me because this was not normal for him, and in prison, anytime something isn't normal, it stands out with flashing lights.

Because of Ruben's odd behavior, and the fact it was obvious the schmuck thought I had dope, I began to ponder what could've possibly led him to believe I had the bag. In order to figure it out, I reversed the surveillance and started to watch what he was doing and who he was dealing with. Then it hit me...

Apparently, Old Man Smiley was getting and selling the black to this schmuck Ruben. Ruben, being the weasel, door sniffin', schemin', Smegal-from-Lord-of-the-Rings type of sheister he is, would pay Old Man Smiley with canteen, then watch to see who Old Man Smiley would give it to. Ruben didn't know Old Man Smiley was actually getting cash from me, then taking the cash to whoever had the dope, working his little twists, dealing with Ruben, and then paying me. So when he saw Old Man Smiley give me the canteen, he automatically assumed I was the one Old Man Smiley was getting the dope from. Like a typical dope fiend, he was sure that he had it all figured out, and in an effort to remove Old Man Smiley from being the middle man – I'm sure he knew Old Man Smiley was getting something from it, and he probably figured he could get a better deal if he dealt with me directly – he tried to befriend me and propose some kind of network/trade between us. What he didn't know, even to this day I'm sure, is that I really didn't have any dope; although, I'm sure he'll swear to you that I did.

Now, Smiley was a friend of mine. I'm not sure he intentionally used me to throw Ruben off his scent; I think Ruben is just a weasel who kept Old Man Smiley under surveillance until he felt he saw enough pieces of the puzzle to figure everything out. And once he saw Old Man Smiley give me – a man who's relatively quiet and private anyway – the canteen, he was just certain he had uncovered our secret operation. But because he was so "sure" he knew what was going on and perception is reality, the whole thing put me in danger; he was genuinely offended I would not deal with him, and that could have caused him to rat on me.

Of course, I didn't have any dope, and although my cash was well-stashed, even if the officers did find it, the offense is minor, so I wasn't in the kind of danger I would have been had I had dope, it still wasn't not the ideal situation to be in... ya know?

The moral of this story is that, although Old Man Smiley and I are friends and it's likely he wouldn't intentionally use me as a smoke screen; the fact of the matter is, I did serve as his smoke screen. And, even to this day neither Ruben nor I know who actually *was* selling the dope. So, maybe in the end, Old Man Smiley outsmarted us all....

ASHKER

Todd Ashker is a validated member of the bloodthirsty Aryan Brotherhood prison gang. He's been convicted of killing on their behalf. His body is covered in Aryan Brotherhood tattoos such as swastikas, as well as scars from stab wounds and gunshot wounds. He's also a successful jailhouse lawyer. This is his story.

$$$$$

Todd Ashker was born in July of 1963 in Denver, Colorado. His mother raised him and his younger sister largely on her own, working long hours as a legal secretary. Sometimes they would be on welfare, and though his mother did her best, they mostly got by on the bare minimum – no extras of any kind and their clothes were usually from thrift stores.

At a young age, Todd began stealing things he felt he and his younger sister needed. His first memory of stealing is from when he was 6 years old. It was Easter morning and they had nothing to color the eggs with, so he went to the store and stole a coloring kit. At age 8, he was arrested for the first time for stealing toys.

Due to a lack of stability, Todd, his mother and sister moved around often, settling in various housing projects, never staying more than a year. Being the new kid, he was often tested. This resulted in him fighting a lot. And right when Todd would finally make some friends, they would move again and the process would start all over.

By the summer of 1973, Todd and his family moved to San Diego, California. Here he began to participate in sports; of course, stealing most of the equipment he needed because his mother didn't have the money to buy it. But this only lasted a year because his mother also couldn't afford the basic playing costs.

In 1975, Todd's family moved north, to the San Francisco Bay Area. Between the ages of 13-17, Todd was in and out of different juvenile facilities for various property crimes and other small offenses. Despite his difficult upbringing, Todd was an A student until eventually dropping out after the 7th grade. In 1981, however, at the age of 17, he got his GED, just before paroling from the California Youth Authority at the age of 18.

At the age of 19, Todd went to prison for the first time, for burglary. It was during this time that he got his first swastika tattoo. He also got "White Pride" tattooed. When he got out, he only lasted four months before going back to prison, in 1985, for burglary and assault. He was sentenced to six years and sent to Folsom State Prison, which, at the time, was filled with racial tension and gang wars. Meanwhile, Todd's father, Lewis Ashker, murdered a retired police officer in South Dakota during a botched robbery and was sentenced to life in prison.

Blood In

In September, 1986, Todd was charged by Folsom prison officials of assaulting another prisoner and possession of a home-made weapon. This landed Todd in the hole, where he would live in an old cell, roughly 6'x8'. Nine months later, in May of 1987, Todd was assigned the "tier tender" job for his unit, where he would be responsible for mopping the floors in front of the cells. This would allow him extended time to spend out of his cell during the evenings. This did not last long, however. On May 25, Todd was mopping the tier in front of "Dirty" Dennis Murphy's cell. Murphy was, according to prison rumor, a high-ranking member of the Aryan Brotherhood – the "AB" or "Brand" as they are often called. Murphy had allegedly murdered a disabled inmate due to a dispute over a shot of heroin. The AB is a ruthless, bloodthirsty prison gang known for killing prisoners and guards alike, even when in "lockup facilities," such as the hole Todd and Murphy were now in.

Allegedly, while Todd was mopping the floor in front of Murphy's cell, Murphy lounged on his bunk.

Murphy's cellmate, Robert Tanner, was out for a shower. When Tanner returned from the shower and guards opened his door to let him back in the cell, Todd rushed past him and began engaging in battle with Dirty Dennis Murphy. Tanner went in behind Todd, grabbed the mattress off the top bunk, and held it against the doorway to block the guards' view. Guards fired 3 shots into the cell, right through the mattress. When Tanner removed the mattress from blocking the doorway, guards rushed into the cell and removed he and Todd, neither of whom looked to be injured. But Dirty Dennis laid on the floor, where he had been stabbed between 17 and 26 times, depending on what report you read, and shot once in the shoulder. When a guard asked him what happened, Murphy allegedly replied, "Fuck you, punk," then died just minutes later.

When guards searched the cell, they found a prison-made shank with Todd's bloody fingerprints on it. CDC brought the case to Sacramento prosecutors and they charged Todd with 1st degree premeditated murder. The prosecutor assigned to the case, D.A. Bill

Portanova, planned to argue that Todd carried out the hit on behalf of the AB. If convicted, Todd faced 30 years.

Validation and More Bloodshed

While Todd was preparing himself for trial, prison officials began the process of validating him as a member of the Aryan Brotherhood. A year later, in the summer of 1987, they validated him as an "Associate," considered less connected and dangerous than an actual member. They did this while building a case to validate him as an actual member, which they ultimately did on May 23, 1988.

Initially, Todd represented himself for the murder of Dirty Dennis, something prison gang members are known to do because it allows them to oversee subpoenas and witness lists, where they can then call other gang members to court in an effort to execute violence against witnesses and other targets. But after Todd complained officers were sabotaging his defense efforts by searching his cell, the judge appointed attorney Philip Cozens to represent him.

During the trial, which took place in February and March of 1990, D.A. Portanova argued Todd had killed Murphy on behalf of the AB. Todd, however, argued he killed Murphy in self-defense; a strategy, according to federal investigators, the Aryan Brotherhood often uses to justify a murder. According to Todd, Murphy had challenged him to a duel. Todd understood this to mean they were going to fistfight each other and he took no weapons into Murphy's cell. He claimed that when he went into the cell, however, Murphy had pulled out a prison shank made from a sharpened piece of metal cut from a locker. Todd claimed that, when he saw the shank, he wrestled Murphy to the ground, taking the shank from him, where they engaged in vicious combat until the guard shot into the cell, hitting Murphy. The fact that Murphy was a known and vicious member of the AB and Todd was not, at least at the time of the fight, gave merit to the self-defense claim. And Todd called several witnesses who described the chain of possession of the shank: A senior member of the AB cut the metal from his locker prior to the fight, then smuggled it from person to person until it got to Dirty Dennis. AB members testified to this, as well as that Todd was not a member of the Aryan Brotherhood. Todd's lawyer was confident that the jury would find little evidence of premeditation, and thus, at the most, find Todd guilty on the lesser charge of second-degree murder, which carried less time.

Two months into the trial, Todd's lawyer was asked by a *Sacramento Bee* reporter during a lunch break how he thought the trial was going. Strangely, Cozens responded with a cryptic, "Ask for me tomorrow, and you shall find me a grave man" – a quote spoken by Mercutio in Shakespeare's Romeo and Juliet shortly before he was stabbed. Then, around 3pm that afternoon, Cozens entered the hallway of the courthouse where the holding cells were so he could interview John Paul Schneider, a known AB member who goes by the name Cornfed, so he could prepare him to testify as a defense witness. Schneider, 28 at the time, was serving a life sentence plus 11 years for attempted murder after stabbing a guard in the throat, what he allegedly did to gain entry into the Aryan Brotherhood. During this meeting, Schneider began to stab Cozens, hitting him a total of four times with an 8-inch shank; three times in his left arm and once in his leg. Sheriffs saw Cozens bleeding and ran in to subdue Schneider. There, they found the shank, which had been engraved with a shamrock, a symbol used by the Aryan Brotherhood, and covered in blood.

Two weeks later, Cozens filed a motion to recuse himself from representing Todd, telling the court he suspected his client of plotting his murder, creating an obvious conflict of interest. Investigators alleged Todd was frustrated with the way his defiance was going and orchestrated the attack. The presiding judge, James Morris, however, disagreed, and called the evidence against Todd speculation. In addition, he declared that a mistrail or dismissal of Cozens would waste the two months invested into the trial and ultimately reward the

AB for their violence. He offered Todd the choice of representing himself or keeping Cozens, and Todd chose to keep Cozens.

Todd was ultimately found guilty of second-degree murder. The jury was not convinced the murder was premeditated, or that Todd was a member of the Aryan Brotherhood. On April 24, 1990, the judge sentenced Todd to 16-to-life, which was to be added to the sentence he was already doing for burglary. Cozens saw this as a victory, and rightfully so. Years later he would describe Todd as having "a certain ruthlessness to execute other people to advance his agenda."

As a validated member of the AB, Todd was to serve an indeterminate sentence in the Security Housing Unit (SHU). On May 2, less than two weeks after his conviction, Todd was transferred to Pelican Bay State Prison, and new SHU (pronounced "shoe") that had opened in December of 1989, built specifically to house the "worst of the worst," such as California prison gang members like those of the Aryan

Brotherhood, Mexican Mafia, Nuestra Familia, and Black Guerrilla Family.

Welcome to Skeleton Bay

During the early years, Corcoran and Pelican Bay SHUs had a history of setting up gladiator fights, and Todd did not escape this. On October 24, 1990, after he'd been in Pelican Bay for 6 months, Todd's door opened simultaneously with another prisoner's, even though SHU inmates are to be kept apart at all times. Todd and the other inmate began fighting, as gang code dictates, then officer Steve Broudeur shot Todd in the arm with an assault rifle at close range, ending the fight.

The first doctor to examine Todd recommended he receive emergency surgery at a non-prison hospital. Despite this, Pelican Bay doctors put a cast on Todd's arm, sent him back to his cell, and he was written up for "Assault on Inmates." Over the next two months, Todd complained of excruciating pain and requested medical attention but was denied. For two weeks, an aneurysm expanded in his arm before eventually bursting in December, 1990, resulting in Todd being airlifted to a non-prison hospital so he could get the surgery he'd needed for two months.

Todd filed a lawsuit, handwriting a complaint that guards and doctors at Pelican Bay had violated his civil rights. A jury agreed and awarded him $225,000 in damages. This experience introduced Todd to the power of the law and motivated him to earn a paralegal certificate. He has since filed several lawsuits against CDC over medical malpractice and other issues, many of which have been successful.

Despite not receiving any serious writeups, Todd remained in the SHU for the next two-plus decades. As a validated member of the Aryan Brotherhood, prison officials, at this time, were allowed to keep prisoners in the SHU indefinitely. The only way out was to die or debrief – snitch to prison officials, telling them everything you know about your fellow gang members. Doing this, however, will get you on the gang's hit list, and you will be a target for murder. Also because of Todd's gang affiliation, which he continues to deny, he has been denied parole several times, even though he is technically eligible.

The Hunger Strikes

In 2011, to protest long term SHU confinement, Todd collaborated with other long-term SHU prisoners (and documented gang members) on creating the Prisoner Human Rights Movement (PHRM). In addition to the principal negotiators (Todd Ashker, Arturo Castellanos, Sitawa Nantambu Jamaa [Ronnie Dewberry], and George Franco), the PHRM is composed of 20 representitives. The principal negotiators represent over 100k inmates in the 33 California prisons. Representatives and local councils monitor and record conditions at their prisons, which they then report to the principal negotiators.

On April 3, 2011, Todd, fellow AB Danny Troxell and nine others signed a declaration titled "Final Notice." This Notice warned CDC that several inmates in the D-Corridor at Pelican Bay SHU were planning to refuse food indefinitely unless five core demands were met. Among the demands were that they be provided a handball and warm clothes when going out to the yard, where they'd go a few times a week, alone; the ability to make a weekly phone call; adequately nutritious food; and the possibility that indefinite solitary confinement be reviewed periodically. The prisoners drafted the memo by passing kites, shouting through drain pipes, and communicating through advocates in San Francisco.

On July 1, the hunger strike began. Around 6,000 California prisoners participated by refusing all three of their state-issued meals. The movement quickly grew, gaining national and even international media attention. The strike ended on July 20, after CDCR agreed to enter negotiations with the Pelican Bay PNs (Principal Negotiators) and immediately conceded to a few points. However, much of what had been going on did not change. Because of this, the hunger strike resumed on September 26, this time with about 12,000 prisoners in California and other states who participated. It, too, was eventually called off after negotiations seemed to resume properly. However, after negotiations began to stall again, Todd filed a class action lawsuit on May 31, 2012 on behalf of The Pelican Bay Hunger Strike Negotiators and the SHU inmate. The case was an amended version of the earlier suit filed by Todd Ashker and fellow AB Danny Troxell. Judge Claudia Ann Wilken of the U.S. District Court for the Northern District of California presided over the case. Meanwhile, the strike resumed again in July, 2013. This time, Todd and close to 30,000 prisoners in the state of California refused food for over 50 days. Dozens of prisoners were hospitalized and at least one died after hanging himself. The strike ended after a judge issued a court order allowing the strikers to be force-fed by the state. By this time, however, the truth about SHU conditions had been brought to public light. Most Americans had no idea prisoners were being held in the SHU for decades.

As a result of Todd's lawsuit and the efforts of the PHRM and their supporters, as well as a peace treaty created by the gang leaders called the "Agreement to End Hostilities," Judge Claudia Ann Wilken ended indiscriminate solitary confinement in California in 2015. Many of the prisoners who had been in the SHU for decades, including the gang shot callers, were released into the general population. Here, the "peace treaty" would be put to the test....

ONE DAY DEEP

By Steve "Adisa" Champion

December 1982. Five days before Christmas at midnight the Los Angeles County Sheriffs bus lumbers to a stop in front of the oldest penitentiary in California to deposit my codefendant and me after having been sentenced to death. Arriving in the midst of an unrelenting storm, we peer in stark silence out the bus window. San Quentin looms against the dark, its main gun tower rising in the sky like an erection. The prison is a sprawling monolith, foreboding and ugly. A knot in my gut tightens. I have never been to prison. Flashbacks to all the war stories I'd heard in the county jail set off an artillery of images: race riots, stabbings, sadistic guards and hordes of hardcore prison gangs jockeying for power and dominance of the black market. Being tested comes with the territory, so I know I will need to hone my weapon-making skills quickly.

As we exit the bus, we're greeted by a squadron of stone-faced guards clad in green ponchos, brandishing Billy clubs, and eyeing us menacingly. I walk into San Quentin with youth on my side. I am 6' 2", 190 pounds, solid from pumping iron, and vicious from years of gang life. I'm not worried about predators. I'm worried about something much more deadly – the gas chamber.

The rain is coming down hard as we shuffle, flanked by four guards, in waist chains and ankle shackles to R&R – Receiving and Release. The intermittent flashes of lightning seem to underscore my violent life – an amalgam of crime, street wars, juvenile detention centers, and getting high. The single-story R&R building is built of red brick and faces the expansive lower yard. The exterior is nondescript. The inside resembles intake areas of most police stations: there's a long counter for placing your meager possessions, getting fingerprinted, and signing whatever papers they slide in front of you. The smell of disinfectant, urine, funk, and stale tobacco assaults my nose. In two large mesh-wire holding pens, long wooden benches bolted to the floor, a steel sink-and-toilet combo, a barred window, and sloppy graffiti on the walls face each other. In one of the pens a cadaverous buck-naked black guy dances maniacally, happy in his own dementia. He reminds me of Sammy Davis Jr., except for the excrement plastered to his body. Somewhere between my prison mug-shot and being assigned a prison number (which becomes more important than my own name) I learn that at age 20 I am the youngest person on death row. I also learn I'm number 107. I ask the guard what that means. Grinning, he says, "You're the hundred-and-seventh person on the row." I don't find that amusing, but I am curious if it indicates I will be the one hundredth and seven person to be executed. (It doesn't.)

At some point two guards appear and tell us to strip out. We peel out of the flimsy county jail jumpsuit, shoes, socks, and boxers and hand them over one item at a time. The guards toss the clothing in a heap but expertly examine our shoes. Then we're told to "go through the routine" – the most common ritual in every jail: raise your hands to the sky, wiggle the fingers, run them through your hair (if you've got any), stick out your tongue, pull your ears back, lift your nutsack up, turn around and show the bottom of your feet, then bend over and pull your butt cheeks apart. It's over in seconds, though sometimes just to be cruel a guard will make you do it twice.

Once we're processed, my codefendant and I are separated. I'm handed prison blues, tattered wool blankets, dingy underwear, tooth powder, and half a toothbrush – all standard issue fish-kit accoutrements. Then I'm cuffed, arms behind my back, and bookended by two guards. They inform me I am going to the Adjustment Center (AC), where the death-row overflow is housed. Neither of them shouts, "Dead man walking," though one of them does yell "Security escort!" every few feet until we reach AC. I notice no matter where we turn, I am always in clear sight of a gunman 30 feet above my head cradling a Mini-14 carbine rifle. Each of the gunmen nods slightly to my escorts, giving me the creepy feeling I'm being herded along through checkpoints like a bovine to the slaughterhouse.

AC is an unadorned three-story security unit the color of bleached bones. It is a prison within a prison, standing apart from all other units. It sits directly across from the prison chapel. Good and evil locked in a mythic battle: one building for saving souls, the other for destroying them. A large sign with bold red letters hanging next to the entrance cautions: NO WARNING SHOTS FIRED IN THIS UNIT!

Entering AC is like entering a crypt. The huge steel door closes behind me with such finality that I get the claustrophobic sensation of being locked underground. Adrenaline rushes through my veins. The outside belies the interior of AC. There is nothing bright about it. Not the dull piss-colored walls, not the dim fluorescent lights blinking eerily, not the bleak atmosphere. An icy chill tightens my skin, a thick melancholy envelops me. Other than the low hum of

TV sets, the place is as quiet as a morgue. "You're gonna die here," one of the guard's whispers to me. I say nothing.

After I'm strip-searched a second time, we wind our way up a concrete stairwell, squashing cockroaches too slow to scurry away. I'm put in a cell and told someone will come see me in the morning. I scan the small area, then lie on the thin mattress. I stare at the ceiling and begin reviewing my life. For me, violence has become like a second skin, an accepted doctrine upon which I've meditated and which I've carried out with brutal exactitude. Now, for the first time in my life, I look over the carnage. I don't like what I see, and I don't have much hope things will get any better. Tomorrow is just another shitty day in a series of shitty days. I flick off the single 40-watt bulb dangling above my head and close my eyes to put some distance between me and the reality of my future: being choked to death by acid and cyanide.

This was my first day in San Quentin, my first glimpse of the coming madness. Sleep didn't come easy. Still edgy from the long bus ride, I tossed and turned all night without any idea I was only 30 yards from the gas chamber.

$$$$$

Steve "Adisa" Champion is a former Crip from South Central Los Angeles. He has been on Death Row since December 1982. The stories in this book by Steve are from his book *Dead to Deliverance*, a fascinating read about growing up a Crip and life on Death Row. I highly recommend it.

THE CONFESSION

A prisoner serving a life term as California State Prison and Substance Abuse Treatment Facility in Corcoran published his confession to the brutal murder in January 2020 of two convicted child molesters with whom he was housed. Jonathan Watson, 41, sent a letter in February 2020 to the *San Jose Mercury News*, which detailed how he used a cane belonging to fellow prisoner David Babb, 48, and beat him to death, after becoming enraged that Babb was watching children's TV programming in the prison common area. Using the same weapon, Watson then clubbed to death Graham De Luis Conti, 62. All three men were serving life sentences, Watson for first-degree murder and the other two for aggravated sexual assault of a child under 14. Watson's letter claims he confessed to clinical staff he was on the verge of violence and asked them to move him from the housing unit, but the request was ignored.

Meanwhile, life goes on in California prisons….

WINO

Wino is 6'2", 158 pounds. He has tattoos all over his body, including his face, including devil horns tattooed on his forehead. He's a grimy son-of-a-bitch – a dope fiend. He is also very respected and feared – despite looking like a dusty broomstick.

See... Wino built his reputation by knocking people out. Yep; one hit, and they drop. In fact, Wino's also available for hire. If you need to have a dope debt collected, send Wino; all you have to do is pay him a couple of pills.

And he rarely has to ask someone more than twice to pay up. People get nervous just by seeing him approach...

Or, say you want to send someone a message by having them knocked the fuck out; all you have to do is pay Wino a $50 paper of heroin and they'll be laying on the ground the next time he sees them – easy work.

However, although Wino is feared for his massive amount of knockouts, what Wino does to knock people out is blindside them – catch them when they ain't looking or expecting it. Of course, nobody ever mentions that part, because in prison it's all legal; there are no rules except to handle your business. Wino learned right where to hit someone in order to knock them out, and he's not afraid to do it. But, does he really have something special going on, or is that all it is?

One day I saw Wino get confronted by the friend of a guy he'd knocked out. The guy walked up to Wino and politely asked if he could have a word with him. Once he'd pulled Wino to the side where he was away from everyone else; while standing in front of him, face to face, he took off on Wino. BAM! Cracked him, right in his jaw. What did Wino do after the first hit? He fell to the floor and balled up into the fetal position. The confronter then jumped on top of him and pounded his head in about ten more times before getting up and walking away; all 5'4", 146 pounds of him.

After Wino was able to get up, he dusted himself off, looked around to see who saw, then walked away as if nothing had happened. A few days later, Wino and a friend of his had jumped someone, was written up for a battery, and eventually transferred to another prison.

I, too, was eventually transferred to the same prison Wino had been sent. I saw Wino at the new prison, and of course he was back to doing what he does: knocking people out with one hit, being a bully and causing other prisoners fear. Not a lot of people had seen what happened to Wino that day, and most of who did were either still at the old prison, or still afraid of him because of the reputation he'd built over the years by knocking so many people out. You never know, maybe he just had a bad day, a cramp or something, and he's not just a pussy with a menacing paint job (tattoos). Why take the chance, right?

I, on the other hand, happened to not give a fuck about Wino or his knockouts, and he knew that; I could see it in his eyes when he looked at me. Wino also knows that I know about his little secret – what had happened that day at the old prison. Although, I ain't gonna put him on blast or anything...

There are actually two opposing morals to this story: 1) Wino is a pussy that people actually fear, all because of his bluff that he semi-backs up by knowing where to hit someone, and having the nerve to do it. 2) Just because someone has tattoos all over and a reputation for knocking people out (or whatever), doesn't necessarily mean they're all that bad. Peel off the tattoos and look at the substance of the man; and like the 5'4", 146-pound guy, you might just see a nice, soft vagina.

CORRUPTION AT CORCORAN

Corcoran State Prison is one of the most infamous prisons in America. Located in California's central valley, the prison is made up of two main sections: the general population, which houses high-security level 4 inmates (though sometimes this changes), and the Security Housing Unit, also known as the SHU (pronounced "shoe"). Within the SHU, however, is a subsection called "Protective Housing Unit," or PHU, which has housed and houses some of the Golden State's most high-profile prisoners, such as the now-deceased Charles Manson, Robert Kennedy's assassin, Sirhan Sirhan, and others. The rest of the SHU, with the premise of making prison safer by segregating the most violent inmates, houses validated prison gang members, like those of the Mexican Mafia, the Aryan Brotherhood, the Nuesrta Familia and the Black

Guerrilla Family, and inmates who have committed SHU-able rule violations in other prisons, often the soldiers of the prison gang leaders.

It didn't take long for Corcoran to become corrupt after it opened in 1988, especially in the SHU. Almost immediately a group of officers created a gang called "the Sharks," where they would greet busses of new SHU arrivals that they would attack without provocation or warning. These officers would wear black leather gloves to avoid leaving marks on the prisoners they manhandled. "You're at Corcoran SHU now!" they would yell at the arriving inmates who were shackled head to toe and posed little or no threat. "Spread your legs as wide as you can! Look up at the sky and don't move!" I remember them telling me when I arrived there years later, in 2003. "If you move an inch, we will see that as an attack on officers and you will be dealt with accordingly!" they yelled at us.

Like prisoners, these guards created "cars" – cliques – and to impress the older officers – the leaders of the cars – the younger ones would tell them they wanted to "do a bus."

"Once the veteran guys got some dirt on the younger ones, they knew they could trust them," said guard-turned-whistleblower, Richard Caruso. "You bleed in front on me and I'll bleed in front of you and then we can go out and drink together," they would say, according to Caruso.

Shooting Gallery

Things quickly became increasingly violent in the SHU. As early as October of 1989, a few supervisors began to suspect something sinister going on. When it came time each day for SHU inmates to go to the exercise yard – two at a time, 20 to a session – bitter rivals were being put into the cramped space, which is about the size of half a basketball court. There, they would fight, as gang code dictates. This became known as "Gladiator Day." Guards who watched the yard from the tower did so armed with a .37mm gas gun that discharges five small wood blocks and a .9mm carbine rifle. The wood blocks were not meant to kill, but break up fights in which one inmate threatens "imminent great bodily harm" to another. Inmates relied heavily on the knowledge that the first shot was supposed to be from the less lethal gas gun, and they would continue to fight as the wooden blocks flew all around, as this, too, was required by gang code. But if the gas gun did not stop the fighters, the deadlier carbine was to be used. However, guards claimed they were unclear what constituted "great bodily harm," so some would fire wooden blocks at inmates' feet and never pick up the carbine, while others would pick up the carbine almost immediately.

In late 1989, SHU inmates began complaining about being released from their cells out of order by officer and union rep Pio Cruz. Cruz would play roll of fight announcer, calling out the combatant's names as they entered the yard, which became known as the "Shooting Gallery," according to a supervisor who later testified at a 1990 administrative hearing. One morning, after sending two rivals to yard, Cruz ran up to the gun post, took the gas gun from the gunner's hand and fired wood blocks at the inmates. The gunner testified that Cruz then ordered him to lie about the shooting. These gladiator fights would go on to become such events, witnesses would come from other buildings to watch them. Sometimes supervisors would even delay letting the inmates out to fight so that female officers and secretaries from elsewhere in the prison they were trying to impress could arrive. Guards would then bet on the inmates, then shoot them to "break up the fights."

Then, in November of 1989, guards wanted to search the cell of inmate Reginald Cooke. He had spit on a male officer and shown his dick to a female officer. But Cooke refused to come out until an extraction team arrived and forcibly removed him. He put up a small fight but ultimately yielded. The incident appeared over when guards carried Cooke, arms and legs shackled, to the rotunda. But then, with more than twenty officers watching, a lieutenant ordered Cooke's pants to be lowered, then delivered a jolt to his dick with a stun gun. When it came time to report the incident, another lieutenant ordered the extraction team to omit any reference to the taser. Kings County prosecutors tried to investigate the incident, but ran into a wall of silence after the correctional officer's union pressured witnesses not to cooperate.

Mushroom George

Problems worsened in February 1993 when Associate Warden (AW) George Smith was promoted to Warden. In the first six years Corcoran was open, six SHU inmates and one elsewhere would be killed by carbine fire; more killings than any other prison in the country. Four of these fatal shootings would occur in the first fifteen months Smith was Warden. Smith, who staff dubbed "Mushroom George," apparently because mushrooms like to be kept in the dark, liked to turn a blind eye to what was going on. Smith liked to project a tough-guy image and kept pictures on John Wayne in his office. Smith's close ally – his "underboss" – was Associate Warden Bruce Farris. Farris oversaw the SHU.

During this time, fights between Black and Latino inmates became commonplace, especially during second watch, which is 6am to 3pm. According to log books, in one 8-month period in 1994, 85 fights broke out in the 4-A, 4-Left building during second watch, compared to just eight fights during third watch. Steve Rigg, a third watch lieutenant from 1988-1994, who eventually cooperated with the FBI, became convinced that the second watch officers were staging fights. He had overheard second watch supervisors betting on outcomes, and these officers would move rivals next to each other to make it easier to justify letting them out together. Rigg and his third watch crew would move the prisoners apart from each other, but when the second watch came back the next day, they would undo the moves. "I told my sergeant to unstack the tiers so that the known enemies wouldn't be released to the same yard," Rigg said, "but when the second watch would come in the next morning, they would reverse everything I had ordered and stack the tiers again. This happened all the time. I was trying to keep a lid on the violence and they were adding more fuel to the fire. They wanted to create fights. I think they liked shooting at some of the troublemakers.... Gunfire was ringing out nearly every day and these shooting were not justified," he said. According to Rigg, the supervisors involved with the staging of the fights were a group loyal to Smith and Farris.

In April of 1993, just two months after Smith was promoted to Warden, inmate Michael Mullins was shot dead by a SHU guard trying to "stop a fight." At least one captain and a lieutenant had protested that the wrong inmate had been shot.

But even brass wanted in on the shooting action. In early 1994, two lieutenants grabbed a .37mm gas gun from guards and fired rounds at an inmate who refused to return to his cell. According to Rigg, one of them later showed off photographs of the battered inmate.

"They could have used pepper spray on the guy," said Rigg. "Instead, they went in the control booth, took the .37mm and fired seven times, thirty-five projectiles. The guy was tortured, and here's this lieutenant showing off photos and bragging about it."

No action was ever taken against the lieutenant, and a similar incident would happen later.

Headshot

In April of 1994, Pearson Tate, a 25-year-old gang banger from South Central Los Angeles who raped a teenage girl in a funeral home parking lot, and his cellmate, were in the so-called shooting gallery as they awaited two Latino gang members to charge.

Once they did, a brawl ensued, and the gunner shot Tate in the head with a carbine, killing him, supposedly with a bullet meant for his attackers, who were the aggressors, according to the incident report. Lieutenant Rigg felt from the beginning that the fight was set up, as Tate had recently been moved to a cell next to the two Latinos. Rigg also said when he came to work, he witnessed a lieutenant schooling the gunner on how to write his report. Rigg said he learned later that a number of supervisors had gathered in the control booth before the fight, a surefire sign of "Gladiator Day." There had also been a fight earlier that morning between another pair of rival inmates. One of the officers who had come to watch was from another unit. At the last minute, the gunner on duty had been replaced with a more experienced gunner. Despite this, and the fact it was all caught on the security camera, the shooting review board ultimately exonerated the gunner. However, shooting review boards are made up of three officials from other prisons, and according to Captain Simpson, "The shooting review boards are nothing but a rubber stamp. You don't go into another man's house, his prison, and tell him his floor is dirty. You'd be stupid to anger the Warden at Corcoran because at some point he's going to be on the panel to judge your prison." Apparently, the review boards are as stacked as the tiers.

"Mr. Tate was a loudmouth and very disrespectful to staff," said Rigg. "But the man didn't deserve to he murdered."

After the killing, Rigg and a small number of supervisors made several appeals to Warden Smith – Mushroom George – to change the shooting guidelines and not place rival gangsters in the SHU yard together. But Smith refused to budge. "We were having four or five shootings in an 8-hour shift," said Robert Talbot, a lieutenant who retired in 1994. "Officers would tell me, 'Well, boss, we're going to have a war today. So-and-so is going to yard with so-and-so and they're all enemies.' I finally went to my supervisor and said 'These guys are going to fight. We're doing nothing but shooting at them and writing incident reports. It's a lot of senseless bloodshed.' He told me, 'We can't segregate the yard. You know the policy. If they fight every day, so be it. They'll get tired sooner or later.'" Talbot said the guards had a take on every fighter. They knew their fighting styles and abilities and would bet accordingly. "It got so bad that we had medical staff standing by waiting for each incident to happen."

Frustrated, Rigg and Talbot began holding shooting classes to remind officers under their command that serious bodily injury had to be imminent before they could use the gas gun. But Rigg was told to stop the classes. "The Warden chastised me, threatened to fire me," he said.

The Takedown

Rigg decided he needed to find an ally in the gunner ranks, so he picked officer Richard Caruso, a 6-foot-4, 270-pound former Marine police officer who arrived at the SHU in late 1989 and was a part of the "car." Caruso was under investigation for firing a single round of wood blocks at an inmate. Rigg figured Caruso's action was far less severe than what others had gotten away with, so he called him to his office. But Caruso was skeptical because he had filed a grievance against Rigg the day before. "I felt harassed because Rigg was telling me not to use the .37mm," Caruso said. "I told Rigg, 'I don't trust you. You bleed for me and I'll bleed for you.' That's when Rigg reached in a file and pulled out photos of one of the inmates tortured by the .37mm. "Here," he said. "This is what the lieutenant who's going after you did to an inmate. Take them in front of your hearing board and ask them why they are pursuing a case against you and ignoring a case against the lieutenant."

That night, Rigg and Caruso spoke on the phone until 2am about the Tate killing and other shootings they felt were bad. The next morning, Caruso drove to the library and found a newspaper article on the Tate killing. "My jaw dropped," he said. "The prison's press release said that Tate was the aggressor and that he was shot after failing to heed all warnings. Even the incident report said he was the victim."

Rigg asked Caruso to gather files from the prison offices. After doing so, they made plans to go to the FBI. But first Caruso wanted to pay Warden Smith a visit. "I'm here to show my loyalty, George," he told him. Then he told Mushroom George everything he'd done, everything he knew, and everything he'd gathered, including the video tape of the Tate killing, and his plan to meet with the FBI the next morning. "Do you still want me to meet with them?" Caruso asked Mushroom George. Caruso saw tears come to George's eyes. "I think he saw the whole house of cards coming down."

The next morning, two FBI agents knocked on Caruso's door. They told him the prison felt he'd stolen the evidence, and that the state's investigators were on their way with a subpoena. When the investigators arrived, Caruso stepped out with the FBI agents at his side. "Did you give them the stuff?" the investigators asked. "Yeah, I gave them the stuff," Caruso told them. The investigators shook their heads in disgust, then turned around and walked away. Caruso was looked at as a turncoat and transferred to kitchen duty where he was the only officer in charge of several inmates, many of whom did not like Caruso for shooting at their homies in the SHU.

Ralph Mineau, a captain from 1989-1995, would also be one of the officers to cooperate with investigators. According to one prison memo, during a staff meeting AW Farris announced that "Mineau should be shot or killed."

But even as the FBI had Corcoran and some of its top brass in their sights, abuse continued. On June 21, 1995, nearly a year into the FBI investigation, three dozen officers, many of whom were part of the Sharks gang, waited for a busload of Black inmates coming from Calipatria State Prison. Many of the officers wore their black leather gloves and placed tape over their name tags. Apparently, according to a Department of Corrections inquiry, underboss Farris had allowed rumors to spread that the 36 inmates had assaulted guards, and that they were also hiding weapons in their braids and dreadlocks. As the bus pulled into Corcoran, the inmates saw the Sharks doing stretches and warm-up exercises. Then, when the shackled inmates were pushed off the bus, one by one, they were assaulted with fists, batons, and combat boots worn by the guards. Some inmates were poked in the eyes and some had their nuts yanked on while guards called them niggers. Others were rammed head-first into walls and windows. Lieutenants and sergeants joined in and even led the assaults, according to witnesses. To taunt the inmates further, guards took clippers and shaved off their hair and beards. Many of the injuries, including fractures, were not treated for months.

The officers claim they did nothing wrong, but upon the Department's investigation, Farris, Captain Lee Fouch, and Lieutenant Ellis McCant were fired, and five other lieutenants and sergeants were demoted or suspended.

In July of 1996, Mushroom George retired at the age of 60, citing poor health.

Car Crash

Federal charges were ultimately brought against eight officers in February 1998 for conspiring and violating the civil rights of SHU prisoners by failing to keep them safe from harm. Prosecutors allege that 84 fights took place between one 5-and-a-half-month period during the defendant's shift – 300% more than any other unit or shift. The prosecutors focused on two of the fights. Sergeant Truman Jennings and guards Timothy Dickerson, Michael Gibson, and Raul Tavarez were charged with staging a tag-team fight between three SHU prisoners on February 23, 1994. And Lieutenant Douglas Martin, Sergeant John Vaughn, and guards Jerry Arvisu and Christopher Bethea were indicted for setting up the brawl that ended the life of Tate; Bethea was the officer who fired the carbine into Tate's head, killing him. SHU prisoner Anthony James, a key prosecution witness, testified moments before the fight broke out Bethea had bragged it was "duck hunting season." But Bethea claimed he fired the shot to wound the prisoner who was fighting with Tate.

Despite the overwhelming evidence of these crimes, on June 8, 2000, all eight officers were acquitted. Some observers believe the prosecution lost its case before the trial even started, when the seven-man and five-woman jury was impaneled. One of the male jurors had applied to become a prison guard. The late husband of a female juror had been a CDC sergeant. Another female juror worked for the Madera County Jail system, and another was a Superior Court clerk. Hardly the jury you'd want to prosecute prison officials in front of.

None of the guards work at Corcoran any longer. Whistleblowers Rigg and Caruso both went on disability for stress-related problems after finding it impossible to work in any California prison because other guards ostracized them from breaking CDC's mafia-like code of silence.

THE SUMMERR OF BLOOD

By Steve "Adison" Champion

It had been almost two weeks since a sharpened piece of metal was drilled into Lil Lou's 21-year-old cerebellum, extinguishing his existence. Two weeks since the joint went up like a munitions dump, pitting black, brown, and white prisoners against each other in a bizarre ritual where the spilling of each other's blood became pro forma. Two weeks since the Department of Corrections declared a state of emergency: total lockdown – no yard, no showers, no visits. Nothing! It was war, and everyone took sides.

Lil Lou and I were friends, and I didn't take his death lightly. He was killed on his way to broker a "peace treaty" between warring factions of black and Mexican prisoners. It was a classic ambush, and Lil

Lou made a fatal error. He died trying to defend himself armed only with his feet and hands.

What came next was not mere fanaticism but full-blown evil. Like a virulent strain of Ebola, violence wrapped in racial hatred infected nearly the entire California prison population. Men with nothing to lose, cooped up in crackerjack boxes 21 hours a day, couldn't wait to carve their frustration and anger into someone's flesh.

I was no exception.

There are some predictable reactions to particular conditions, and things can quickly spiral out of control. That's what happened the summer of '84 – Vietnam, we called it. Prison wars are never over political ideology; they're about saving face and gaining respect. It is also a common practice for prison guards to instigate racial and gang violence. The aberrant belief is that if inmates are at each other's necks, they won't be focusing on the guards. The divide-and-rule tactic of pitting one group against another as a means of controlling them almost always works because of the racial component.

Men coming into the prison system become conscious of their skin color in a way they never were before. You quickly become pro-black, pro-white, or pro-brown. The racist attitude of some of the white prisoners and the white guards who sympathized with them made it easy for me to adopt a Black Nationalist attitude. Prison culture is so racially divided, it looks worse than the segregation era. It compels you to ride with your group whether you belong to a gang or not. There is an unwritten law that says: whenever there is a racial war you are obligated to "get down"; otherwise, you will be immediately branded as a punk or a traitor.

Two weeks after Lil Lou's death, the casualty rate at San Quentin was climbing. Although there had been killings and assaults on both sides of the war, the primary injuries were due to "spearing" or "gassing." Spearing is the use of a makeshift spear (blade attached to a pole) to stab someone through the cell bars as he passes by. Gassing is having a hot liquid thrown on you – usually a mixture of boiled hair grease, water, and urine. There are also the occasional prison-made zip-guns and incendiary devices that can have lethal effects. There were also guys "cutting out," using hacksaw blades and jewelers' wire to saw the bars off their cells, then squeezing through the opening and whacking someone entering or exiting his cell. Any weapon can be made or invented, and prisoners are geniuses when it comes to hurting each other.

Whenever someone had a blanket or sheet blocking the view into their cell, or a puddle of soapy water on the ground (this was meant to slow you down), you had to be extra alert because all it took was a fraction of a second to be blow-darted or speared. I had no intentions of getting hurt. I followed my own security measures religiously. It was a survival strategy, and failing to adhere to it could have cost me my life.

During the lockdown, one hot meal and two sack lunches were passed out every day. It was up to you to make them last. The blacks refused to allow anyone on the tiers who was suspected of collaborating with the enemy. Guards passing out food wore face shields and were accompanied by another guard holding up a large Plexiglas shield to protect both guards against objects being thrown at them from prisoners.

One morning a phalanx of guards came in the unit to search for weapons. I was told they found contraband in my cell. The next day an arrogant guard came to my cell and sarcastically said, "Pack your shit. You and some of your buddies are being moved." Since he didn't give us a reason, we refused. We knew in C-Section there were racist guards (working in conjunction with racist prisoners) who were setting up blacks to be stabbed. It was wartime and we weren't going to be easy targets. When we got no explanation, we prepared for cell extraction. What we called the "goon squad" (the prison internal gang unit) was called in to surgically remove each of us. They came suited and booted: batons, Kevlar vests, tasers, mace, stun guns, and Plexiglass shields bigger than Captain America's.

While we waited for them, Evil (Steve's co-defendant, Anthony Ross, one of the founders of Raymond Avenue Crips) told Big Bub to get ready – to fill his sink with water and hold up his mattress to prevent being tasered and maced. Richard was next door to me, so I told him to do the same thing. I cut two adjacent lines in my mattress so I could slide my arm through and hold it like a shield. When the extraction squad came on the tier, we were ready.

"Cuff up!" the fat lieutenant barked.

"Fuck you!" was our collective response. Big Bub was cell extracted first, then Richard, me, and Evil. Each extraction lasted a few minutes or so. When they got to my cell I could see they were huffing and puffing from the fight Richard had given them.

"What the fuck you waiting for, come on with it," I yelled.

I was pumped up. But they waited for their wind to come back. Finally, they opened the door slowly and five of them rushed in – crashing the shield against the mattress I was holding. That was the contact I waited for. I dropped the mattress, jumped on the bed and went gladiator on them. I hit everything in sight. I knew it was just a matter of time before they took me down. I finally got wrestled to the floor, and that's when they took their shots. They hit me several times in the body, and the fat lieutenant kept trying to taser me after I was handcuffed, so I tried to knee him in the nuts. Three guards lifted me off the ground and slammed me hard against the wall.

When they dragged me out of the cell and took me downstairs, some fool gassed me with an unknown substance, probably hot piss, but my adrenaline was so high I didn't even feel it. The guards escorting me started laughing, so after I was put in another cell and uncuffed, I spit a glob of snot into one of their faces. "Now laugh at that, mothafuckah," I told him. He stopped laughing.

By the end of June, we were still locked down. Much of my frustration stemmed from not being able to fight like I wanted to. During the search, the guards had seized everyone's property. We were left with one blanket, one sheet, one pillow, and no toiletries. Nearly weaponless, we were reduced to mainly throwing hot water and piss. The war became a joke. There was no victory for anyone. The prison administration modulated everything in our environment: food, water, mail, space, toilet paper, even the clothes we wore. We all knew this, but nobody gave a fuck. We just continued to try to maim each other.

Every morning all the blacks would exercise. It was our way of maintaining discipline and morale. I would call the cadence "Can't stop!" And all the blacks would respond "Won't Stop!" This echoed throughout the building. The blacks in D-Section, which was directly behind C-Section, would follow suit with a similar exercise program. Through the chaos and lockdown, I saw many guys mature and some mentally break down. They witnessed a lot, and war changed them.

Many guys were eventually transferred to other prisons and a game of musical chairs was played inside San Quentin. Prisoners were moved from block to block so they couldn't become ensconced in one place.

Some guys welcomed the change because it kept them out of the line of fire. There was one guy who locked himself inside his cell. He made ropes from braided sheets and tied them to and through his cell bars, around his toilet and bed. His theory: he wasn't coming out, and no one was getting inside his cell.

Eventually the violence petered out, not because anyone called a truce but, like in any war, because practicality necessitated it. There were still skirmishes whenever someone got caught slipping, but for the most part violence died out because wars in prison are always ephemeral. They are quick bursts of fury and rage that you learn to ride out, hopefully without getting killed.

So there I was, two weeks after Lil Lou entered the afterlife, on the second tier, slick with sweat and with a bandana tied over my nose and mouth. I'm standing at my cell bars half-naked, in boxer shorts and tennis shoes, coughing on the stench of two weeks' worth of smoldering pillows, magazines, newspapers, and human waste. Thick bluish smoke is anchored in the air like ozone, making it difficult to breathe. It's some extremely noxious stuff, probably toxic. I'm looking down at a foot of garbage and rubble strewn on the first tier. I see several fires from the night before. Though small now, they continue to burn despite being just a pile of dark humps. About half a dozen emaciated brown rats make their way through the mess, like refugees picking through the aftermath of war.

I'm standing there thinking about the insanity of prison and how it ultimately leaves you scarred. I'm thinking about how you have to fight back paranoia and how it takes a ton of work just to keep the mental hinges from springing apart. I was standing there with a five and-a-half-foot spear that rainforest Indians would have been proud of. I was waiting for an enemy to walk past my cell.

SKS

One of my good friends, who for the purpose of this story I'll call SKS, is a real, true, dedicated-for-life hustler/criminal. I mean, SKS did not use any kind of drug, but he loves the thrill he gets from committing crimes and hustling. He loves the cat-and-mouse game with the correctional officers, and even more so he loves beating them. Put it this way: you can give SKS five million dollars to just go on living comfortably, but he'd still smuggle in drugs and/or anything else he's not supposed to have, but can hustle.

SKS is an extremely charming guy. Everybody likes him, including most correctional officers. He just has a fun, outgoing, energetic, and, believe it or not, caring personality. He's real sociable and talks to any and everybody – whites, blacks, browns, officers, free-staff, etc.; if you're within ear range, you can get some conversation. However, he is also very slick, devious, cunning and manipulative. He's a true Machiavellian.

One time, SKS pulled a semi-famous broad off the Internet and she began to visit him every weekend. Not only did she visit him every Saturday and Sunday, she gave him all the money he wanted, when he wanted it and how he wanted it. However, SKS wanted her to do more than just visit and give him money, he wanted her to bring him in drugs; not drug to use, of course, but drug to hustle on the prison yard. And, despite of not being in any need of money, it wasn't long before he had her smuggling in contraband like tattoo ink, cash, cologne, tobacco, pictures of her pussy, drugs, etc. – whatever else he could fit into his asshole.

Now, it wasn't enough that she was bringing him in shit to smuggle from the visiting room to the prison yard. No, that's not at all enough for SKS. He didn't only have to hustle and beat the correctional officers, but he had to do it right in front of their faces.

It's risky to keister things in the visiting room because there are usually several cameras. Rather than look around the room to see who's doing what, the visiting officers that sit at the podium will usually look at a monitor showing various camera angles. Furthermore, they usually have some kind of joystick-type-thing that allows them to point the cameras and zero in on any specific table. So, basically, you never know when you're being watched, because although the correctional officers aren't looking directly at you, they might be watching you via camera.

The risk factor doesn't stop there. The cameras record what's going on in the visiting room, and occasionally the prison's crime squad will review the recordings to see if anybody has been doing anything they're not supposed to be doing. So, it's not only very important that you don't get seen by the correctional officers at the podium, but that you don't get recorded by the cameras, either. Aware of all this, here was SKS' solution...

When it was time for SKS' broad to make the pass and him to keister the contraband, they didn't try to hide in a corner, be slick behind another visitor, or do it any other logical way one might think of doing it, they did it in a way and at a time when it was least expected – at the podium, in front of the officers. That's right, they hid in plain sight.

What they'd do is walk up to the podium and chat with the officers. The podium comes up to about the bottom of one's chest, so that blocked the front view from the officers. And if any camera in the back of the room was directed at the podium, it couldn't catch anything because their backs were to it. The cameras may have been able to record and be aimed at specific targets, but they don't have X-ray capabilities. So the pass would take place in the thin space between the front of their bodies and the podium.

Now, how/when/where would SKS put the contraband in his ass? By sticking his hand down the front of his pants to keister the goods, right there in front of the officers while talking to them, at a time when they least expected it! Yep, while the officers and cameras were focused on the guys in the corners of the room who were trying to hide from view, the guy who was bringing in more contraband than anyone on the yard was right there in front of their faces, sharing a few laughs. Of course, we all knew what SKS was really laughing about, as well as who got the last one...

TOOKIE

The Crips is one of the biggest, most violent and feared street gangs in America. Since its creation in 1971, countless bodies have dropped as a result of the Crip's gangland activities. But from the savage streets of South-Central Los Angeles, where it all started, the Crips have also become a household brand; a part of pop culture, like movies and hip-hop, where some of the biggest rappers, like Snoop Dogg, Roddy Ricch, Jeezy and Lil Baby claim membership.

This story is about one of the co-founders of this notorious gang – Stanley "Tookie" Williams – and his journey from gangster to anti-gang advocate.

$$$$$

Stanley "Tookie" Williams was born in New Orleans, Louisiana on December 29, 1953 to a 17-year-old mother. By the time he was a year old, his father had abandoned them.

In 1959, Tookie and his mother hopped on a Greyhound and headed to Los Angeles in search of a better life. They settled in an apartment, in South Central, an area Tookie would later describe as "a shiny red apple rotting away at its core."

While Tookie's mom worked several jobs to support them, he became bored at home and began wandering the streets. He started to hang out in abandoned houses and vacant lots where he'd watch adults get drunk, abuse drugs, gamble, and fight dogs. Tookie would be paid a few bucks to water, feed, and patch up dogs who'd been mauled in the battles.

Eventually, the adults who were fighting the dogs began encouraging Tookie to fight other kids, where the adults would bet on who would win. If Tookie won, the gamblers who bet on him to win would split their proceeds with him. He began beating the other boys to unconsciousness and developed into a skilled street fighter. Because Tookie was an out-of-towner, he was often the target of neighborhood bullies, street thugs, and older kids who were in local gangs. By the age of 12 he began carrying a switchblade for protection, but by the time he was a teenager, his reputation as a skilled fighter began to grow, and this earned him an enormous amount of respect in the streets.

In the mid to late 60s, juvenile crime increased in South Central as older gangs disband to join groups within the Black Power movement, such as the Black Panthers. Violent youth gangs began to form in their place, which Tookie despised as predatory, but because of his viciousness, ability to fight and willingness to fight the older youth without hesitation, they respected him. At age 15, after befriending a local teen named Donald Archie, who went by "Doc" or "Sweetback," he was invited into a small West Side clique, and soon earned the clique's respect after kicking the ass of one of its members for insulting his mother. Leadership was not chosen but determined naturally, and Tookie became the unofficial leader of his clique as his rep for violence grew.

In 1969, at the age of 16, Tookie was arrested in Inglewood for car theft and sent to Los Padrinos Juvenile Hall in Downey, California. While doing time there, the facility's gym coach introduced him to Olympic weightlifting. This experience sparked an interest in bodybuilding for Tookie, and by the time he was released in 1971, he was much bigger and stronger. Reportedly, when he was asked by the review board what he was going to do when released, he told them he was going to be "the leader of the biggest gang in the world."

Shortly after Tookie's release, he was approached by Raymond Washington, a gang leader from the East Side of South Central who had heard of Tookie's toughness and willingness to fight members of larger, more established street gangs such as the L.A. Brims and the Chain Gang. What Tookie noticed first about Washington, other than him being incredibly muscular, was that Washington and his crew dressed similar to

Tookie and his crew, wearing leather jackets, starched Levi's jeans and suspenders. Washington proposed that they use their influence in their perspective regions to form an alliance in an effort to provide its members with protection against others who would prey upon weaker cliques. This alliance became what is now known as the Crips.

At the time of the Crips initial formation, there were only three subgroups – or "sets" as the Crips would call them – within the larger Crip collective: Washington's East Side Crips (known today as the East Coast Crips), Tookie's West Side Crips, and the Compton Crips, which was led by local teenager Mac Thomas. Together, these guys went on an aggressive campaign to recruit the local cliques into the Crips gang. To do this, they would challenge the leaders of the cliques to one-on-one street fights. Most of these cliques agreed to join the Crips with their subgroups becoming a set within the larger Crips collective. The Crips quickly became the biggest gang in South Central, both in size and territory. However, many gangs resisted becoming a member of the Crips. These hold-out groups ended up banning together and calling their alliance "Bloods." The Bloods would become the Crips' main rival. The L.A. Brim and the Chain Gang, who Tookie grew up fighting, joined the Blood alliance and became The Brims and the Inglewood Family Bloods, respectively.

As leader of the West Side Crips, Tookie became the archetype of the new wave of L.A. gang members who would engage in random acts of violence against rival gang members and innocent people alike. Tookie and his ace, Curtis "Buddha" Morrow, would noticeably participate in these activities, pumping fear into other street thugs, but also the residents of South Central, Watts, Inglewood, and Compton. Soon, the Crips began to morph into what they initially banded together to fight against. "We started out – at least my intent was to, in a sense, address all of the so-called neighboring gangs in the area and to put, in a sense – I thought 'I can cleanse the neighborhood of all these, you know, marauding gangs.' But I was totally wrong.

And eventually we morphed into the monster we were addressing," Tookie would later explain.

Tookie's violent acts became legendary in South Central's underworld. "I was always known for being a fighter. When I was beating people, I made sure they knew it was Tookie who was hitting them. I was a megalomaniac and wanted my gang to be the biggest in the world. At first it was all about fighting, but then the Crips became too big to fight so the other gangs started shooting," he says. And this is when things took an even worse turn.

On February 23, 1972, Curtis "Buddha" Morrow was shot to death following a petty argument. "People started dying, friends of mine, but you never think it's going to happen to you. The thing that makes people most dangerous is when they start believing they are invincible."

Then, in 1974, Raymond Washington was arrested for second degree robbery and sent to Tracy prison, where he'd serve five years. Shortly after

Washington's arrest, Mac Thomas was murdered under "mysterious circumstances."

Around this time, Tookie began to live a double life. He got a legal job working as an anti-gang counselor in Compton, while still serving as the boss of the Crips. He studied sociology at Compton College during the day, then participated in violent attacks against the Bloods during the night.

In 1976, Tookie was shot by the Bloods in a drive-by while sitting in front of his Compton house. He dove to the ground to avoid being hit, but was shot in both legs. He was told by the doctors that he'd never walk again, but after a year of physical rehabilitation and an intense workout regimen, he regained his ability to walk. However, he also started to use drugs again, including smoking PCP. Drug use had been a problem for Tookie since about the age of 12, when he befriended a neighborhood pimp who would pay him money and drugs, particularly Quaaludes, barbiturates and weed, in exchange for running errands for him. Also in 1976, Tookie's grandmother died. They were very close, and her passing was extremely hard on him. With all of this, his life began to unravel.

In 1977, Tookie was fired from his counseling job after being implicated in a robbery committed by two youth from the group home in which he supervised, and he was denied an opportunity to compete in an amateur bodybuilding contest after it was discovered he was a gang leader. Things began to take a mental toll on him, and after a bad trip on PCP, he was admitted to a psychiatric ward for a brief stay. With each of these challenges, Tookie began to use even more PCP, and to support his habit, he would intimidate and rob drug dealers in South Central.

By 1978, the Crips had grown to roughly 45 different sets, numbering 20,000 members in L.A. county alone. And they were no longer just fighting over turf, they were involved in the production and distribution of drugs and other crimes, and they were willing to kill whoever got in their way. And though Tookie and Washington were the founders of the Crips, they had only nominal control over the activities of the various "sets." The Crips fought rival gangs such as the Bloods, but Crip sets just as often fought each other.

The Murders

According to prosecutors, on February 28, 1979, late in the evening, Tookie met with a man, documents identify only as Darryl. Tookie then introduced Darryl to other friends of his – Alfred "Blackie" Coward and Bernard "Whitie" Trudeau. Shortly after the meeting, Darryl and Tookie got in Darryl's brown station wagon and drove to the residence of James Garret. Coward followed in his 1969 Cadillac. Tookie often stayed at Garret's house and kept some of his belongings there, including a shotgun. After about ten minutes, Tookie returned with the shotgun and the men drove to the home of Tony Sims, in Pomona, where they discussed places to rob. The four men then went to another residence where they smoked PCP. While there, Tookie left and came back with a .22 handgun, which he put inside the station wagon. Tookie told Coward,

Darryl and Sims they should hit a spot in Pomona. Tookie and Darryl got into the station wagon and Coward and Sims got into the Cadillac. They got on the freeway and got off on Whittier Boulevard.

The men pulled up to the Stop-and-Go market. At the request of Tookie, Darryl and Sims went inside the store to rob it. Darryl was strapped with the .22 Tookie had put into the car earlier. Johnny Garcia, the clerk at the Stop-and-Go had just finished mopping the floor when he saw the men pull up. When he entered the store to serve them, he saw one man go down one of the isles while the other approached him and asked for a cigarette. Garcia gave him a cigarette and even lit it for him. After three or four minutes, the men left the store without robbing it. Reportedly, Tookie was upset that the men had not carried out the robbery and told them they would find another place to rob, where they would all go inside so he could "show them how to do it."

Coward and Sims followed Tookie and Darryl to a 7-Eleven on Whittier Boulevard, where the store clerk,

26-year-old Albert Lewis Owens was sweeping the store's parking lot.

When Darryl and Sims entered the store, Owens put the broom and dustpan down and followed behind the men. Tookie and Coward, however, followed behind Owens. When Darryl and Sims walked to the register to take the money, Tookie reportedly took a shotgun from under his jacket and pointed it at Owens' back and told him to "shut up and keep walking," where he then escorted him to the back storage area. Once inside the storage room, with the shotgun still at Owens' back, Tookie reportedly said, "Lay down, muthafucka."

Coward would later say that he heard the sound of a round being jacked into the chamber, then a shot, followed by breaking glass, where Tookie had shot Owens in the back at very close range. The men ran off after netting around $120 and headed back to Los Angeles. Once back in L.A., Tookie asked the men if they wanted to get something to eat. According to reports, when Sims asked Tookie why he shot Owens,

Tookie responded because "he was White and he was killing all White people." Later that day, Tookie allegedly bragged to his brother Wayne about killing Owens, saying "You should have heard the way he sounded when I shot." Tookie then made gurgling sounds and laughed hysterically.

According to prosecutors, a few weeks later, on March 11, Tookie alone, at around 5am, entered the Brookhaven Motel in South-Central Los Angeles holding a shotgun, then broke down the door that led to the office, where he then shot and killed 76-year-old Yen-Yi Yang; his wife, 63-year-old Tsai-Shai C. Yang; and their daughter, 43-year-old Yu-Chin Yang Lin, immigrants from Taiwan who ran the motel. He then emptied the cash register and left, netting about $100. The Yang's son, Robert, who was asleep with his wife in one of the motel rooms, was awakened by the sound of someone breaking down the door to the office. Shortly after, he heard a scream from a female, followed by gunshots. Robert entered the office and saw that his mother, father and sister had been shot, and the cash register was empty. The forensic pathologist later testified that Yen-Yi Yang suffered two close-range gunshot wounds, one taking chunks out of his left arm and abdomen, and the other one to the lower-left chest. Tsai-Shai also received two close-range wounds; one to the tailbone, and the other to the abdomen, entering at the naval. Yu-Chin Yang Lin was shot once in the upper-left face area from just a few feet away. Witnesses would later testify that Tookie referred to the victims as "Buddha-heads."

Ultimately, police investigations of these murders and the earlier Owens killing led to the arrests of Tookie and several other gang members. This same year, after Washington was released from prison, he was shot and killed in Los Angeles. His murder was blamed on the Hoover faction of the Crips, which led to a war between the Hoover and other Crip factions.

Tookie stood trial, and although he maintained his innocence, in 1981 he was found guilty on four counts of capital murder in Los Angeles Superior Court, as well as two counts of robbery. The judge sentenced him to death, and on April 20 of that year, he was sent to San Quentin's Death Row, becoming CDC# C-293000.

Tookie in Prison

When Tookie arrived to prison, he was angry and defiant. He was constantly fighting with inmates and guards alike. He was disciplined for threatening to have several guards and their families killed, and he once threw a chemical in a guard's face that resulted in the guard being taken to the hospital for burns. Another time, Tookie was seen engaging in sexual activities with a female visitor. When a guard ordered them to stop, Tookie allegedly threatened to have the guard killed. On another occasion, according to guards, they learned that Tookie had ordered fellow Crip inmates to kill another inmate. The man was attacked and stabbed, though he survived. For these offenses and others, in 1987, Tookie was placed in the hole, also known as solitary confinement, where he would go on to spend almost seven years. While in the hole, however, Tookie began to reflect, and he began to have both a change of thought and heart. "It didn't happen overnight," he later explained. "There was no epiphany. It took seven years of solitary confinement, of soul-searching, to realize what I had become and that I didn't want to be that person anymore." Tookie had found religion and repented in the eyes of God. He set course to repair the damage he'd done.

Crip Redemption

In 1994, Tookie was released from the hole. He began using his time to speak out against gangs and gang violence. With his new mindset, he began writing a book, and in 1996, with the help of co-author Barbara Cottman Becnel, he published the first of eight *Tookie Speaks Out Against Gang Violence* anti-gang books aimed at children. The next year, he wrote an apology letter for his role in creating the Crips. "I am no longer 'dys-educated' (disease educated). I am no longer part of the problem. Thanks to the Almighty, I am no longer sleepwalking through life," he writes.

By this time, when the Crip co-founder was asked what he most regretted in life, he simply stated, "Creating the Crips."

However, by 1999, the Crips had expanded for beyond California to the Pacific Northwest, the Midwest, and the east coast, with an estimated 50,000 members. It was considered to be the deadliest gang in America.

In 2001, Tookie published *Life in Prison*, a memoir of his life on Death Row. The purpose of the book was to warn kids away from following his life of crime. "To get a feel for what it's like to live in a prison cell, test yourself," he writes. "Spend 10 hours – nonstop and alone – in your bathroom at home, which is probably about the size of a cell. Lock yourself inside with no more than a radio, a blanket, a book or a magazine, and a couple of sandwiches. To quench your thirst, drink tap water from the sink. You can talk to your family members through the door, but don't open it. Even if you're hungry, thirsty, lonely or tired, don't open the door. When your 10 hours are up, think about the fact that I have spent approximately 150,000 hours in prison cells less clean and less comfortable than your bathroom."

In 2002, Mario Fehr, a member of the Swiss Parliament, nominated Tookie for the Nobel Peace Prize in recognition for his work against gang violence. Although he did not win the award, many supporters spoke out in his favor. He would go on to be nominated for the prestigious award a total of six times.

That same year, the U.S. 9th Circuit Court of Appeals upheld Tookie's conviction. But in a rare move, the panel urged then-governor Gray Davis to consider commuting the death sentence to life behind bars due to his anti-gang work/efforts.

In 2004, Tookie helped create the "Tookie Protocol for Peace," a peace agreement for one of the deadliest and most infamous gang wars in the country between the Crips and their rival, the Bloods. Tookie received a letter from George W. Bush commending him for his actions, and Bush awarded him with a national "Call to Service Award," given to those who help make their local communities a better place to live. Many community leaders pleaded with Bush to pardon Tookie, but that was not possible because he was convicted in a state court, not a federal one, and only the California governor could pardon Tookie. That same year, Tookie released his book *Blue Rage, Black Redemption: A Memoir*, and it was turned into a TV movie titled *Redemption: The Stan Tookie Williams Story*, starring Jamie Foxx.

In November of 2004, when Tookie was promoting the book, he was interviewed by UK journalist Tony Thompson, who visited him in prison. Thompson described visiting Death Row as a "sobering and regulated experience." He explained that, when walking the path to the visiting room, you see a tall metal chimney which, when lethal gas was the preferred method of execution, vented poisoned air from the death chamber into the atmosphere – killing any passing birds in the process. And that, next to the chimney is a metallic structure with two lights, one green, one red. The green light is permanently on; the red only appears when the execution chamber is in use, switching back to green once the prisoner has been pronounced dead. During the interview, which took place in a steel cage that sits in a larger steel cage, where he was only able to take notes on a napkin, Tookie explained to him that, "When I was young, prison seemed like a great place to be. And that attitude continues. Rap stars and other musicians often use the fact that they have been to prison as a way of boosting their credibility. I remember being a kid and people coming back from prison and showing us pictures of themselves and other inmates in the exercise yard. They would be all huge, toned and muscled and that's how I wanted to be. You end up thinking this is a place for real men but that's just not the case at all. This is a terrible place to be."

He also explained his concept behind his protocol for peace.

"Within the prison system rival gangs have agreed to make peace for the purpose of survival. That same philosophy can be transmitted to rival gangs out on the streets. Instead of killing each other, that energy can be harnessed to oppose poverty, illiteracy, unemployment, discrimination and other social and judiciary injustices. The protocol is intended to be simple and straightforward. You don't need to understand Euclidean geometry to work it out. It's all there in black and white to stop the killing, to address the social emergency of urban violence, to stop the madness."

"The message is simple: don't join a gang. All you will find is trouble, pain and sadness," says Tookie. "I know. I did."

Tookie garnered support worldwide for his efforts to stop gang violence. He received more than 50,000 emails from young people, parents and law enforcement officers around the world testifying that his writings have changed and saved lives. "The part I love most is working with young people," he says.

"That's the absolute highlight of my day." Tookie would often mentor kids over the prison telephone.

Surprisingly, Tookie, who had always denied involvement in the murders, makes little reference to the details of his case in any of his books. To this he simply says, "I won't stand on the shoulders of children to argue my innocence."

On October 11, 2005, the U. S. Supreme Court denied Tookie's petition for Writ of Certiorari, which asked the high court to review the lower court's ruling in his case. In early November, Tookie's attorneys filed his formal petition for executive clemency, as well as a motion to obtain new evidence.

However, though Tookie garnered a lot of support, not everyone was on his side. In mid-November, talk show hosts John and Ken of *The John and Ken Show* on Clear Channel's KFI Radio in Los Angeles started a "Tookie Must Die (For Killing Four Innocent People)" hour on their show daily until the execution of Tookie. In the hour, they interviewed advocates on both sides of the issue and expressed their support of the impending execution. To support Tookie, his friend, co-author and political collaborator, Barbara Becnel, helped spearhead campaigns to stop the execution. These campaigns were joined by celebrities, including Snoop Dogg, who appeared at a clemency rally wearing a shirt advertising the Save Tookie website. Jamie Foxx, noting that Tookie's execution date was set for his birthday, publicly stated that the only birthday present he wanted was clemency for Tookie.

On November 29, the American Civil Liberties Union of northern California announced that more than 175,000 Californians had signed a petition requesting the temporary suspension of executions in California until the California Commission on the Fair Administration of Justice could complete its study, due for December 31, 2007. The "California Moratorium on Executions Act," AB 1121, was scheduled to have its first hearing in January, 2006. Press conferences and rallies in more than a dozen California cities called for the halt to all executions and asked Governor

Schwarzenegger to commute Tookie's death sentence to life without parole.

On November 30, the California Supreme Court refused to reopen Tookie's case in a 4-3 decision.

With Tookie's appeals denied, his options to argue and request clemency, to change his death sentence to life in prison without parole, was running out. By December 2005, it had come down to a decision by then-governor Schwarzenegger, who, ironically Tookie had met in the 1970s while working out in Venice Beach.

On December 8, Governor Schwarzenegger held a one-hour closed-door meeting to hear whether or not he should grant Tookie clemency. Tookie's defenders and prosecutors each had 30 minutes to argue their case. A crowd of both Tookie supporters and proponents of capital punishment congregated outside the State Capitol building in Sacramento.

Lora Owens, the stepmother of Albert Owens made a statement expressing what she thought of Tookie. "I think he is the same cold-blooded killer that he was then and he would be now if he had the opportunity again." Owens' two daughters, who was eight and five years old at the time of the murder, were also against clemency for Tookie and they expressed that they were shocked when they learned that their father's killer had been nominated for a Nobel Peace Prize. Governor Schwarzenegger described the decision whether or not to grant clemency as "the toughest thing when you are a Governor, dealing with someone's life."

Interestingly, on December 9, Linda Owens, Albert Owens' widow, issued a statement in support of Tookie's efforts to bring an end to gang violence and his call for peace between gangs. "I, Linda Owens, want to build upon Mr. Williams' peace initiative. I invite Mr. Williams to join me in sending a message to all communities that we should unite in peace. This position of peace would honor my husband's memory and Mr. Williams' work."

On December 11, the California Supreme Court denied Tookie's request for a stay of execution.

Tookie's supporters made another plea directly to Governor Schwarzenegger to stay the execution.

The clock ticked for four days as Tookie awaited the Governor's decision. Then it came.

On December 12, 2005, Governor Schwarzenegger denied clemency for Tookie. He summarized by basing his denial of clemency on the "totality of circumstances." One of those circumstances, however, was "the dedication of Williams' book *Life in Prison* casts a significant doubt on his personal redemption...the mix of individuals on [the dedication] list is curious... (b)ut the inclusion of George Jackson on the list defies reason and is a significant indicator that Williams in not reformed and that he still sees violence and lawlessness as a legitimate means to address societal problems." With all forms of appeal exhausted, Tookie was scheduled to die the very next day.

The Execution

Thousands of people protested outside San Quentin on December 13, most of whom were seeking Tookie's clemency. I was incarcerated during this time (as I am still), and I remember Corcoran State Prison, where I was at, going on lockdown as the administrators feared something may happen as a result of Tookie being executed.

Hours before the execution, Tookie was interviewed by WBAI Pacifica radio where he stated: "My lack of fear of this barbaric methodology of death, I rely upon my faith. It has nothing to do with machismo, with manhood, or with some pseudo former gang street code. This is pure faith, and predicated on my redemption. So, therefore, I stand strong and continue to tell you, your audience, and the world that I am innocent and, yes, I have been a wretched person, but I have redeemed myself. And I say to you and all those who can listen and will listen that redemption is tailor-made for the wretched, and that's what I used to be... That's what I would like the world to remember me. That's how I would like my legacy to be remembered as: a redemptive transition, something that I believe is not exclusive just for the so-called sanctimonious, the elitist. And it doesn't – is not predicated on color or race or social stratum or one's religious background. It's accessible for everybody. That's the beauty about it. And whether others choose to believe that I have redeemed myself or not, I worry not, because I know and God knows, and you can believe that all of the youths that I continue to help, they know, too. So, with that, I am grateful... I say to you and everyone else, God bless. So, take care."

Tookie was escorted to the execution chamber. According to witnesses, the mood in the execution chamber was somber and Tookie showed no resistance. After he was strapped to the gurney, he struggled against the straps that held him down and looked up at the press galley behind him to exchange glances with his supporters. He then rested his head on the gurney while medical technicians began inserting needles in his veins. CNN would later report that staff had difficulty inserting the needles, which caused the usually short process to take about 20 minutes. John Simerman, reporter for *Contra Costa Times* reported that "They had some trouble with the second IV, which was in the left arm... Williams, at one point, grimaced or looked almost out of frustration... at the difficulty there... He had his glasses on the whole time. He kept them on, and he kept looking..." With a look of frustration on his face, Tookie reportedly asked the technicians, "You guys doing that right?" A female guard whispered to him, and the second guard patted his shoulder as if to comfort him. It's said that Tookie shed a single silent tear, but otherwise showed no emotion as he was executed.

At 12:35am, Tookie was pronounced dead.

According to MSNBC anchor Rita Cosby, members of the Owens family who witnessed the execution were stony-faced. However, Lora Owens appeared to be very upset. According to Kevin Fagan, a reporter from the *San Francisco Chronicle*, Tookie's advocate Barbara Becnel and two other supporters, a man and a woman, yelled after the execution as they were heading out: "The state of California just killed an innocent man!" Barbara later stated, "We are going to prove his innocence, and when we do, we are going to show that Governor Schwarzenegger is, in fact, himself a cold-blooded murderer."

Rest in Peace

On December 19, Tookie's body was laid out for viewing, drawing 2,000 mourners. A memorial service was held in L.A. on December 20, where Becnel read his final wishes. Tookie's funeral filled the 1,500-seat Bethal AME Church and drew a variety of people, from gang members to celebrities. At his funeral, the last words of Tookie echoed from a tape recording to mourners, whom he asked to spread a message to loved ones:

"The war within me is over. I battled my demons and I was triumphant.

"Teach them how to avoid our destructive footsteps. Teach them to strive for higher education.

Teach them to promote peace and teach them to focus on rebuilding the neighborhoods that you, others, and I helped to destroy."

Six months later, Barbara Becnel and Tookie's longtime friend Shirly Neal carried out Tookie's final wish when they sprinkled his ashes into a lake in Thokozani Park in the city of Soweto, South Africa.

THE INDICTMENT

On May 21, 2019, a 143-page federal indictment was filed that described criminal violations allegedly committed by Ronald Yandell, Daniel Troxell, William Sylvester, Travis Burhop, Brant Daniel, Donald Mazza, Pat Brady, Jason Corbett, Matthew Hall, Samuel Keeton, Michael Torres, Jeanna Quesenberry, Kevin McNamara, Kristen Demar, Justin Petty and Kathleen Nolan.

The indictment detailed an investigation by the Drug Enforcement Administration, the California Department of Corrections and Rehabilitation (CDCR) and "assisting agencies" into the Aryan Brotherhood (AB) gang in California's prison system, and crimes allegedly committed between 2011 and 2016. The defendants were variously charged with Conspiracy to Engage in a Racketeer Influenced Corrupt Organization, Conspiracy to Commit Murder, Conspiracy to Distribute and Possess with Intent to Distribute Methamphetamine and Heroin, Distribution of Heroin, and Distribution of Methamphetamine. Some of the defendants could face the death penalty.

The indictment stated that AB members "Conducted extensive, widespread, organized, criminal activity from within California's most secure prison environments." It said contraband cell phones were used to coordinate distribution of drugs not only within California but in "South Dakota, Missouri, and elsewhere." The illicit cell phones were also used to "orchestrate violent crimes," including murder plots, "both inside and outside of California's prisons," and to arrange smuggling of other contraband. The indictment further described murders committed by AB members, including photos of bloody weapons and crime scenes.

Interestingly, several pages of the indictment were spent blaming a settlement in a federal lawsuit for changes in CDCR's policies on housing dangerous gang members in solitary, specifically California's Security Housing Units (SHU). The settlement, in a 2015 case filed by AB members Todd Ashker and Danny Troxell, was blamed for creating "a growth opportunity" for the gang, because it "required Aryan Brotherhood members to be released from Pelican Bay SHU." Since that time, "the enterprise has experienced a significant resurgence within California's state prisons."

The indictment explained how at least one defendant was a direct beneficiary of the settlement, and how another defendant, Kevin McNamera, an Orange County, California attorney, allegedly met with prisoners to deliver contraband under the guise of attorney-client meetings. Defendant Petty worked for Golden State Oversight, a company the provides quarterly care packages to prisoners, and reportedly conspired to smuggle contraband in package items.

"What we report today is a very significant setback for one of California's most notorious prison gangs," said U.S. Attorney McGregor W. Scott. "The geographic scope of these prison murders and ordered murders extended the length of California, from Imperial County in the south to Lassen County in the north, inside prison walls and out."

SHORTY

Let me tell you a story about a guy I know who, for the purpose of my story, I'll call "Shorty."

Shorty is a dude who is around 40 years of age, and is a menacing 5, foot 2 inches tall. He has a few muscles, but they are like midget muscles. He's basically a little, short, buff, stocky dude – if that makes any sense.

Anyway, despite being the shortest guy on the yard, people actually feared him. Why? Because Shorty was known for making very big metal knives and having them buried all over the prison yard.

Shorty built a reputation for always having big metal pieces close by and ready for action. Everybody on the yard knew it – even the correctional officers. Every so often, the correctional officers would run a metal detector over the grass area and find one of

Shorty's metal pieces. They'd suspect it was Shorty's, but could never prove it because they didn't actually *see* him burying it. People – prisoners and correctional officers – would talk about the discovery, and it would just enhance Shorty's reputation. The prisoners and correctional officers feared Shorty because of the big, nasty metal shanks found in the ground from time to time.

Because Shorty built this reputation, he was respected and feared, despite being the shortest guy on the yard.

One time, the *biggest* prisoner on the yard, a 265-pound buffoon who thought he was some type of shot caller, called Shorty a "coward" because of some dispute they had. However, when he did so, Shorty immediately busted him right in his mouth, drawing blood. The big buffoon was *literally* spitting blood out of his mouth!

Stunned by Shorty's quick reaction, the big buffoon went on a rage talking about how Shorty was "going to pay." However, a couple of hours later, the big dummy went up to Shorty and apologized. Why? Because the big dummy is a typical bluffer, like most bullies, and although he tried to act hard-core, deep down inside he didn't want to take it so far as to start playing with knives – what Shorty had built his reputation as being about.

So the smallest prisoner on the yard, Shorty, punched the biggest prisoner in the mouth for calling him a coward, and the big buffoon ended up doing nothing but apologizing to Shorty – all because of the reputation Shorty built by hiding big nasty knives around the yard.

Now, did Shorty really want to go around stabbing people? No; of course not. Did Shorty want the correctional officers to occasionally find knives on the yard? Absolutely. Every time the correctional officers would find a knife, it would remind everybody about what Shorty was into. What's crazy is that, some of the knives found didn't even belong to Shorty, but people would *assume* they were his. And would Shorty deny that they were his? Yes, he would. But he would intentionally do it in a way where you would think he was lying and just trying to cover up his crime. However, in truth, he *wanted* you to assume they were his.

During the three and a half years I was on that yard with Shorty he never stabbed one prisoner. In fact, besides punching the big buffoon one time in the mouth, I never even saw him get in one fist fight. Was Shorty really a man-stabbing beast trying to kill everything in sight? Fuck no.

I ended up leaving that yard and going to the hole after being accused of slicing somebody. Three months later, Shorty went home.

The moral of the story? Despite being the shortest prisoner on the yard, Shorty had a great bluff game, and it worked for him. I respect it. He pulled it off nicely, and in the end, he made it home.

BOXER

He climbed his way up to the top floor of the Mexican Mafia: La Eme – a bloodthirsty California prison gang which originated in the mid-1950s. His body is covered in Mafia tattoos, including a life-size black hand with the letter "M" inside of it (the symbol of the Mexican Mafia, La Eme), over his heart. He commanded over tens of thousands of Latino soldiers from Southern California street gangs, also called Sureños, who were both on the streets, and in prison. He stole, robbed, trafficked drugs, ordered killings, and murdered people with his own hands, all in cold blood.

Then, in 2002, he turned on the gang he helped mastermind; he became a federal informant and began exposing the Mexican Mafia's deepest secrets.

His name is Rene "Boxer" Enriquez, and this is his story....

$$$$$

Rene was born on July 7, 1962, and grew up in a middle-class home in Cerritos, California. He was a bright kid who showed promise, but he decided to drop out of school in the 9th grade. At age 12 or 13, he got jumped into Artesia 13, a local street gang that his older brother, Marc, who Rene idolized, was a member of. To gain membership, members of the gang took Rene behind a gas station and "jumped" him in – they beat him so he could prove he was fearless, an initiation process used by many street gangs. Marc gave Rene the nickname "Boxer," and from there, he began investing his energies into the gang. His dad tried to keep him on track by making him work in the family business, but Boxer preferred to run the streets, steeling with his friend, Johnny Mancillas, and breaking into nearby homes. He eventually ended up in juvenile hall, after he and two others raped an intoxicated woman at a party.

Like most gang members, Boxer idolized those who'd been to prison. "And once we got into the gangs, we understood that the homeboys that got out of prison were well respected. You go there, and you learn prison," Boxer would later say. "We wanted to get to prison somehow. And we were destined to get there." It wouldn't be long before Rene "Boxer" Enriquez got his wish of going to prison. Arrested for a string of robberies, he was sentenced to several years in prison, where at the age of 19, he was introduced to members of the Mexican Mafia. They took him under their wing and taught him the ways of La Eme. He learned how to make "shanks" – prison-made knives – and hide them in his rectum. He began carrying out "hits" – prison stabbings – for the Mafia, in San Quentin and Folsom prisons, working his way into their good graces. In 1985, he became a "made" man – an official member of the Mexican Mafia; a membership and commitment that is expected for life, as the only way out, is death.

In 1989, Boxer paroled from prison, where he immediately put his membership with the Mexican Mafia into action. He began extorting the local Latino street gangs – the Sureños – and others who made their money off of crime, like selling drugs. He made it clear to those within his territory that you will follow the laws set by the Mexican Mafia, or die. One suspected drug dealer, Cynthia Gavaldon, was thought to be withholding taxes she was ordered to pay, so Boxer ordered her assassination. His next act of terror was to murder fellow Eme member David Gallegos, who had lost favor with the gang after running from a gun fight. To kill Gallegos, Boxer gave him a fatal shot of heroin, then, to ensure he would die, shot him five times in the head. Boxer was eventually arrested and held for trial in Los Angeles County Jail.

Despite incarceration, his reign of terror didn't stop. In 1991, while awaiting trial for the murders, Boxer and another man stabbed Mexican Mafia member Salvador "Mon" Buenrostro 26 times in a lawyer's interview room. Luckily for Buenrostro, he survived. Boxer was ultimately sentenced to three life sentences – one for each murder, and one for the stabbing of Buenrostro.

Boxer returned to prison in 1993. Prison officials wasted no time in validating him as a member of the Mexican Mafia, giving him an indeterminate "SHU" (Security Housing Unit), and sending him up to Pelican Bay State Prison – the infamous SHU facility on California's remote north coast. There, inmates spend 23 hours a day in a windowless cell, and are only allowed one hour a day in a small, concrete "yard," where they can walk around for exercise. Boxer would later say of arriving at the infamous "prison of prisons": "What impacts me immediately as I walk in, is the smell. I just stepped outside from the bus and you smell the pines, the redwoods, the forest... these earthy, loamy smells. But as soon as you step into the SHU, it hits you like a wave. It's the smell of despair, depression, desperation. This is a place where people come to die."

Pelican Bay was designed to isolate and break the members of California's most powerful and violent prison gangs, like the Mexican Mafia, but instead, the gangs turned it into "headquarters." They worked around the isolation by passing gang messages via kites (small prison notes), visitors, and legal mail – mail that guards aren't allowed to read. They used the time to scheme and organize. They taught themselves how to communicate using sign language, so they could do so at a distance when the opportunity presented itself, without the guards hearing, and they learned languages like Nahuatl, an ancient Aztec dialect, so guards couldn't understand them. They created their own codes and messaging systems through which they could pass information, like gang hits, without outsiders understanding their meaning. Boxer Enriquez became one of the criminal masterminds of the Mafia, and there wasn't much of anything anyone could do to stop it. "[Enriquez] had a level of sophistication in conducting his business that it was almost impossible to pinpoint and nail down exactly, everything that he was doing," says Robert Marquez, a special agent with the California Department of Corrections and Rehabilitation. Chris Blatchford, a Los Angeles journalist who often reports on gangs agrees that Boxer was more sophisticated and ruthless than other gangsters. "He was greedier than they were and he was smarter than they were and he really lived off the booty he took from other crooks," Blatchford says.

Enriquez certainly thinks of himself as smart. "I believe I'm a cut above the rest," he would later say with the typical arrogance of a Mexican Mafia member. He describes participating in something called "The Thousand Concepts." "We'd spin off a thousand ideas. And if only one of them was profitable, we were succeeding. So, we'd do this every day up in Pelican Bay, a thousand miles from our base of power, spinning off ideas that paid money."

It's said that one of Enriquez's greatest ideas and Mafia contributions was when, in the mid-90s, he convinced the Mafia to back his idea to order a stop on drive-by shootings on the streets of Southern California. This wasn't done for peace, however; it was done for business. "Our true motivation for stopping the drive-bys was to infiltrate the street gangs and place representatives in each gang, representatives which then, in turn, tax illicit activities in the areas," he says. "And we already had it planned out that California would be carved up... into slices, with each member receiving an organizational turf."

Not so fast, says others. "Boxer wasn't the mastermind behind stopping the drive-bys. Joe Morgan was," says Armando "Chunky" Ibarra, who I co-wrote *Loyalty & Betrayal: My War with the Mexican Mafia (Special Deluxe Edition)* with. Chunky was once an associate of and hitman for the Mexican Mafia, who now has him on their hit list. "Boxer did capitalize on it, though, and I don't say this to undermine the power he did have with La Eme," he adds.

Regardless of who the original creator of the idea was, the plan worked. "Tens of thousands of gang members adhered to what we said. Us. High school drop outs," Enriquez says. "But we had so much authority behind who we were, they listened."

The Mafia had so much power and influence, they were able to make the Sureños fear disobeying their orders. Gang members who commit crimes know they'll eventually end up in prison, where the Mob rules, and any disobedience would make you a target for murder.

The Mexican Mafia's decision to put a stop to drive-bys came with an added benefit, however: it was good PR. "They [La Eme] saw that as a way to being more respectable, in the eyes of sympathetic do-gooders, city leaders, church leaders," says journalist Chris Blatchford.

The success of all this only confirmed to the Mobsters just how much power and influence they had, and how much money could be made without ever touching a drug or pulling a trigger, all from their prison cells, thousands of miles away in Pelican Bay, by outsourcing the work to their Southern soldiers.

"We could do all this; we could become a true powerhouse, because of the finances generated by taxation: taxation, extortion, protection," Enriquez said.

Drug and other illicit profits flowed from the streets to prison, to the accounts of the Mexican Mafia members, by the tens of thousands, right under the nose of authorities. The Mobsters treated the street criminals like owners of a fast-food franchise, using the brand of the Mexican Mafia, and their protection, in return for a portion of the profits. The Mafiosos were pulling in thousands and investing the money into things like bank CDs and government bonds. But, with more money comes more problems, and power struggles began to arise between Mob members. They began fighting over turf and profits, and plotting to murder one another. And when a Mafioso can't get to you, they'll murder those closest to you: a family member. The success fueled greed and paranoia, and the treachery was a turn-off for Enriquez. "This arbitrary targeting of families – because I am your adversary –

takes it to a whole different realm of violence. This was not part of the bargain. This is not the Mexican Mafia that I joined," he says. He got disillusioned, and tired. "Mob fatigue," he calls it. In addition, he had reached the top floor of the Mafia, accomplishing all that one could; yet, when he looked around, even with all the money and power he'd gained, he was still locked in a California prison cell, where he was to remain until he died.

So, in 2002, after close to 10 years in isolation, he decided to switch sides.

$$\$\$\$\$\$$

Enriquez contacted the IGI (Institutional Gang Investigators) and let them know he was "done" – he wanted out of the Mafia. They quickly moved him to a different section of the prison, called Protective Custody, because as soon as word got out he'd defected, the Mafia would put a hit out on him – they'd want him dead, ASAP.

In California, when a validated member of a prison gang, such as the Mexican Mafia, Nuestra Familia, Aryan Brotherhood, or Black Guerrilla Family, drops out, they must go through a debriefing process. This is where the prisoner must tell IGI their entire gang history, every crime they've committed, and everything they know about the gang they are dropping out from. In other words, they must snitch. The debriefing process is one way investigators determine how serious the prisoner is, or isn't, in their decision to be done with the gang. After all, once you snitch, there is no going back.

Because of Enriquez's status and amount of participation in La Eme, when he made contact with IGI notifying them he was ready to switch sides, they could hardly contain their excitement. "For the first time, we had a Mexican Mafia member defect that was really able to lay out for us how the organization works, the organizational structure," said Marquez. Some say Enriquez is the highest-level member of the Mexican Mafia to ever work with law enforcement.

Within a year, the same cops who Enriquez hated, had become his protectors, even "his friends."

Enriquez put the same dedication into his new partnership with law enforcement that he had with the Mafia. After he finished debriefing, he spent most of his time in undisclosed jail locations, where his FBI handler, assigned to facilitate his informant work, oversaw fairly permissive communications with family, reporters, and the public. Enriquez had access to a computer and could make phone calls. He assisted the FBI by listening in on wiretaps and decoding Mafia messages. He led conferences and training sessions for law enforcement all over the U.S. He worked merely full-time as an FBI informant and testified in more than a dozen trials as an expert witness. He appeared in public in a suit and tie. He even got married to his longtime sweetheart and was allowed contact visits.

Enriquez delivered a devastating blow to the Mafia he helped organize and build. For his troubles, the FBI and ATF paid him $200 a week.

Then, in September of 2014, after 10 good years of high-level snitch work, the true test of all Enriquez's hard work and cooperation with law enforcement came about: a parole hearing – his first chance to be released from his 3 life sentences. Officials with at least 11 federal and state law enforcement agencies wrote letters to the Parole Board in support of Enriquez. Several even attended the parole hearing and listened to the Board ask the toughest of questions.

The Board: "Why did you repeatedly participate in criminal activity?"

Enriquez: "[I] lacked… the qualifications to diagnose myself... I could sit here and... guess as to what I was looking for... I don't know what it was."

The Board: "Why did you commit a forceable rape in 1985?"

Enriquez [crying]: "[I] had an understanding that what I was doing was wrong at the time... I wasn't the man I am today and I lacked that social awareness at that time."

The Board: "Why did you join a street gang?"

Enriquez: "[I was] forced."

In the end, the Board granted parole. Now it was up to then-Governor Brown to decide whether or not to uphold the Board's decision, as he had the final say.

Although Enriquez had become somewhat of a public figure by this time, for some reason the Board's decision to parole him was not reported anywhere. From when the Board grants parole, they have up to 120 days to set a prisoner's release date. For Enriquez, this happened in January of 2015 sometime. This, too, received no news coverage. With no denial yet from the Governor, Enriquez began making his plan to parole, where, upon his release, he would enter the FBI's Witness Protection Program.

On January 28, a week or so after receiving his release date, the Los Angeles Police Department hosted a private dinner party for local police chiefs and business executives, where Enriquez, though still incarcerated, would appear as the keynote speaker. They touted him a "criminal corporate executive" who would give first-hand insight to the group about the inner-workings of the criminal enterprise, where he would detail "gang franchising, marketing, sales, merchandising and branding" to the little over 100 attendants. To put on the rather extravagant event required hundreds of hours of law enforcement's time and effort, to plan and get Enriquez there safely. The fancy gathering was reported on by news outlets like the *Los Angeles Times*, *NBC*, and others, all who expressed surprise that so much time, energy, and presumably money had been put into a public event featuring an admitted Mafia murderer – a "convicted hit man," were the words. Nobody knew that Enriquez had actually been granted parole by the Parole Board, and the "convicted hit man" was expecting to be released in just a matter of weeks, something which seems like may have been kept under wraps intentionally.

Something didn't smell right to reporters, so a couple of them decided to dig a little deeper into the situation, and on January 31, the *Los Angeles Times* ran an article about what they'd discovered: Enriquez had been granted parole, and was only awaiting a final decision by Governor Brown. Other local newspapers began following the case more closely, even tracking down the children of one of Enriquez's victims, who expressed outrage over Enriquez's possible release. They also published just how much the January 28 event had cost taxpayers – $22,000. This press was not good for Enriquez.

Then, on February 20, the last day in which he could weigh in, Governor Brown released his review of the Parole Board's decision, where he stated in part: "Mr. Enriquez presents a shallow understanding of how he came to perpetuate so many violent crimes." Brown noted how Enriquez claimed to have found meaning from his "career" in law enforcement, but had admitted to lapsing back into drug use when "not being used by law enforcement." Brown wrote, "Because he is a high-profile dropout targeted by the Mexican Mafia, Mr. Enriquez's parole poses a serious security risk to him, his family, his parole agents, and his community in which he is placed."

Brown's decision to the Parole Board's recommendation: Reversed.

Ironically, part of what Governor Brown used against Enriquez was that he's on the Mexican Mafia's hit list – a result of him dropping out of the gang and cooperating with authorities, something prison officials encourage, even demand, as a part of one's rehabilitation. What law enforcement's reason for supporting Enriquez in being granted parole was at least one of the reasons Brown, who had the final say, used for denying it. One can't help but wonder if the Mafia "mastermind" was, in the end, used, played – checkmated.

Whether or not Enriquez will ever be paroled has yet to be seen. In 2017, the Parole Board granted Enriquez parole again, and on November 2, 2017, Governor Brown denied it again. In early 2019 the Board granted Enriquez parole once more, but in 2019, now-Governor Gavin Newsom denied the decision, saying in part: "I encourage him to continue down his path of self-development and insight. However, given his current risk to public safety, I am not prepared to approve his release."

As of now, Enriquez remains in prison, though on a Sensitive Needs Yard (SNY), where other dropouts and prisoners wishing to avoid California gang politics are housed. Here Enriquez has many more privileges than he did when in the SHU. It is unknown if he is still working with the FBI and other law enforcement agencies.

As for what will happen next? Well, in a story with so many twists and turns, I guess we will just have to wait and see....

BODY PARTS

On March 20, 2020, the mother of a man murdered at the California State Penitentiary, Corcoran filed a lawsuit against CDCR officials, whom she alleged were responsible for the murder of her son. Her son was decapitated on March 9, 2019 by his cellmate, who had previously attempted to murder a cellmate and whose lengthy history of violence rendered him unsuitable for housing with another prisoner. He decapitated her son and made a body-parts necklace.

CDCR prisoner Luis Romero was transferred from another prison to Corcoran, which has a lengthy history of violence. According to a court document, instead of following the usual procedure of having a committee of prison administrators find appropriate housing for Romero, taking into consideration whether a potential cellmate was an appropriate fit, and having both prisoners sign forms agreeing to be housed with one another, they simply placed him in a cell with Jaime Osuna, a prisoner with a lengthy history of extreme violence.

While in jail, Osuna had attempted to murder his cellmate. His continuing violent misconduct had resulted in his being housed without a cellmate since his arrival at CDCR seven years earlier. Further, the CDCR allegedly had documentation provided by Osuna's own lawyers and medical team "warning CDCR of his propensity for extreme violence, insatiable desire to kill, and need to be held in a psychiatric ward, not a prison with other inmates." Qsuna was serving a no-parole sentence for the torture-murder of a woman. He also was known to collect "trophies" of his violent acts.

That night, guards allegedly failed to perform safety checks on Osuna's cell even when a sheet was stretched across the bars, blocking their view.

During the night, Osuna tortured and decapitated Romero. He was found in the blood-covered cell wearing a necklace of Romero's body parts. Romero's body showed signs of extreme torture, all of which was done with a weapon Osuna made from a small razor blade and string.

Meanwhile, life goes on…

EXECUTION DAY

By Steve "Adisa" Champion

It doesn't matter if on the day of an execution, the morning forecast is sunny and warm. A turbulent storm is brewing on the inside, and humidity on death row is always high. The feeling is both eerie and sickening, as if some mysterious, awful sore is about to discharge itself.

Execution day is the quietest day on death row. The usual early-morning banter, pots and pans being hustled about by guards preparing to serve breakfast, the morning ritual of "roll call" as someone shouts good morning to friends, sounds of TVs and radios being switched on – all are stilled. The impending doom sucks sound right from the air.

The silence on the row can be deafening. On any other day, silence is a welcome break from the monotony of the screeching noise. One would assume the silence is a result of people becoming more introspective, more contemplative about the reality of their situation. In some cases, this is true, but the opposite is more likely. Most people are in bed asleep trying to escape. Anytime there is a scheduled execution the entire prison, including all programming, comes to a complete halt. Everything ceases while San Quentin moves into high security, standing patient and poised to snuff out another life. Prison officials stroll the tiers, peering into the cells at us as if they're seeing some rare and disgusting animals on the verge of extinction. They never look you directly in the eyes, perhaps for fear you'd see right through them. Many of them support the death penalty and gleefully rejoice when we are pronounced dead. Nothing is exchanged during these observations but hostile glances.

Most people on death row will be glued to their TVs or radios listening intently as news reporters interrupt daily programming to give updates on the pending execution. The gathering of anti- and pro-death-penalty groups will assemble in front of the prison gate with picket signs and a conviction that their cause will prevail. Like serfs protecting the fortress of their feudal lord from invasion, a phalanx of prison guards standing in full combat gear will form a prophylactic shield in front of the prison gate.

The attorneys for the condemned man will be scurrying around throughout the day, both in front of cameras and behind the scenes, making last ditch efforts to save the life of their client. They'll work overtime trying to convince us that there is always hope, that we should not give up. But we who have been on death row know this to be a lie, because a last-minute appeal to an apathetic court or a politically driven governor (who rode into office as a pro-death penalty candidate) is like asking a hungry, angry bear not to bite you.

Death penalty opponents will give fiery and spirited speeches throughout the night, trying to create a hopeful and optimistic atmosphere in the face of something diabolical. The tug-of-war between the death penalty supporters and opponents will rage on, but in the end no one wins. A reporter will announce the menu of the condemned man's last meal, and the small separate gatherings of true believers and preachers of hate will stand juxtaposed. The silent prayers and candles of the night vigil are as loud as thunder and as bright as lightning.

Death-row prisoners are attuned to everything going on. We understand that whatever the outcome, our situation is amplified. None of us is exempt from the execution, none of us walks away unaffected, and many of us stay up to the last minute, hoping the attorney unearths some new evidence that will alter the court's ruling or, in a temporary fit of idealism, hoping a judge who acted too hastily in an earlier decision will change his ruling. We are always disappointed. But hope, as fleeting or false as it may be, is all we have in this situation.

Men who normally don't pray will find themselves asking God to exert his powers and intervene to save a life. We usually get our answer just after 12:01 a.m. when the person has been pronounced dead. We're then let off lockdown and the prison program returns to business as usual. And we are aware of the routine, which Anthony Ross has vividly described in his essay "Routines":

Four guards in black fatigues will escort you from the death cell to the chamber. A spiritual advisor, if you want one, can accompany you. Once you enter what used to be the gas chamber the guards strap you onto a gurney. The executioner locates a vein and sticks in an IV. When he's finished, he'll look at the warden for a signal at which point the warden will ask you if you have any last words. You may or may not choose to speak. The warden then nods to the executioner who releases 5 grams of sodium pentothal via a 60cc syringe into your bloodstream. In no more than 60 seconds this knocks you out cold. The IV is then flushed with saline and 50cc of alcuronium bromide is sent through the line. This drug will paralyze every single muscle in your body except for the heart. Breathing slows as the muscles controlling the rib cage and diaphragm begin to freeze up. The IV is again flushed with saline and the final poisonous chemical, 50cc of potassium chloride, is pumped into your body. This blocks the electrical impulses to the heart, stopping it from beating. The results: your lungs are imploding, your organs are writhing, and your brain is gasping for oxygen. The outward appearance will look uneventful, but internally all hell is breaking loose. Death comes in less than 15 minutes, but not always. There will be nothing peaceful about it. The warden will announce the time of your demise. The world will move on.

THE CELL BLOCK

BOOK SUMMARIES

MIKE ENEMIGO is the new prison/street art sensation who has written and published several books. He is inspired by emotion; hope; pain; dreams and nightmares. He physically lives somewhere in a California prison cell where he works relentlessly creating his next piece. His mind and soul are elsewhere; seeing, studying, learning, and drawing inspiration to tear down suppressive walls and inspire the culture by pushing artistic boundaries.

THE CELL BLOCK is an independent multimedia company with the objective of accurately conveying the prison/street experience with the credibility and honesty that only one who has lived it can deliver, through literature and other arts, and to entertain and enlighten while doing so. Everything published by The Cell Block has been created by a prisoner, while in a prison cell.

THE BEST RESOURCE DIRECTORY FOR PRISONERS, $19.99 & $7.00 S/H: This book has over 1,450 resources for prisoners! Includes: Pen-Pal

Companies! Non-Nude Photo Sellers! Free Books and Other Publications! Legal Assistance! Prisoner Advocates! Prisoner Assistants! Correspondence Education! Money-Making Opportunities! Resources for Prison Writers, Poets, Artists! And much, much more! Anything you can think of doing from your prison cell, this book contains the resources to do it!

A GUIDE TO RELAPSE PREVENTION FOR PRISONERS, $15.00 & $5.00 S/H: This book provides the information and guidance that can make a real difference in the preparation of a comprehensive relapse prevention plan. Discover how to meet the parole board's expectation using these proven and practical principles. Included is a blank template and sample relapse prevention plan to assist in your preparation.

THEE ENEMY OF THE STATE (SPECIAL EDITION), $9.99 & $4.00 S/H: Experience the inspirational journey of a kid who was introduced to the art of rapping in 1993, struggled between his dream of becoming a professional rapper and the reality of the streets, and was finally offered a recording deal in 1999, only to be arrested minutes later and eventually sentenced to life in prison for murder... However, despite his harsh reality, he dedicated himself to hip-hop once again, and with resilience and determination, he sets out to prove he may just be one of the dopest rhyme writers/spitters ever .... At this point, it becomes deeper than rap .... Welcome to a preview of the greatest story you never heard.

LOST ANGELS: $15.00 & $5.00: David Rodrigo was a child who belonged to no world; rejected for his mixed heritage by most of his family and raised by an outcast uncle in the mean streets of East L.A. Chance cast him into a far darker and more devious pit of intrigue that stretched from the barest gutters to the halls of power in the great city. Now, to survive the clash of lethal forces arrayed about him, and to protect those he loves, he has only two allies; his quick wits, and the flashing blade that earned young David the street name, Viper.

LOYALTY AND BETRAYAL DELUXE EDITION, $19.99 & $7.00 S/H: Chunky was an associate of and soldier for the notorious Mexican Mafia – La Eme. That is, of course, until he was betrayed by those, he was most loyal to. Then he vowed to become their worst enemy. And though they've attempted to kill him numerous times, he still to this day is running around making a mockery of their organization .... This is the story of how it all began.

MONEY IZ THE MOTIVE: SPECIAL 2-IN-1 EDITION, $19.99 & $7.00 S/H: Like most kids growing up in the hood, Kano has a dream of going from rags to riches. But when his plan to get fast money by robbing the local "mom and pop" shop goes wrong, he quickly finds himself sentenced to serious prison time. Follow Kano as he is schooled to the ways of the game by some of the most respected OGs whoever did it; then is set free and given the resources to put his schooling into action and build the ultimate hood empire...

DEVILS & DEMONS: PART 1, $15.00 & $5.00 S/H: When Talton leaves the West Coast to set up shop in Florida he meets the female version of himself: A drug dealing murderess with psychological issues. A whirlwind of sex, money and murder inevitably ensues and Talton finds himself on the run from the law with nowhere to turn to. When his team from home finds out he's in trouble, they get on a plane heading south...

DEVILS & DEMONS: PART 2, $15.00 & $5.00 S/H: The Game is bitter-sweet for Talton, aka Gangsta. The same West Coast Clique who came to his aid ended up putting bullets into the chest of the woman he had fallen in love with. After leaving his ride or die in a puddle of her own blood, Talton finds himself on a flight back to Oak Park, the neighborhood where it all started...

DEVILS & DEMONS: PART 3, $15.00 & $5.00 S/H: Talton is on the road to retribution for the murder of the love of his life. Dante and his crew of killers are on a path of no return. This urban classic is based on real-life West Coast underworld politics. See what happens when a group of YG's find themselves in the midst of real underworld demons...

DEVILS & DEMONS: PART 4, $15.00 & $5.00 S/H: After waking up from a coma, Alize has locked herself away from the rest of the world. When her sister Brittany and their friend finally take her on a girl's night out, she meets Luck – a drug dealing womanizer.

FREAKY TALES, $15.00 & $5.00 S/H: *Freaky Tales* is the first book in a brand-new erotic series. King Guru, author of the *Devils & Demons* books, has put together a collection of sexy short stories and memoirs. In true TCB fashion, all of the erotic tales included in this book have been loosely based on true accounts told to, or experienced by the author.

THE ART & POWER OF LETTER WRITING FOR PRISONERS: DELUXE EDITION $19.99 & $7.00 S/H: When locked inside a prison cell, being able to write well is the most powerful skill you can have! Learn how to increase your power by writing high-quality personal and formal letters! Includes letter templates, pen-pal website strategies, punctuation guide and more!

THE PRISON MANUAL: $24.99 & $7.00 S/H: *The Prison Manual* is your all-in-one book on how to not only survive the rough terrain of the American prison system, but use it to your advantage so you can THRIVE from it! How to Use Your Prison Time to YOUR Advantage; How to Write Letters that Will Give You Maximum Effectiveness; Workout and Physical Health Secrets that Will Keep You as FIT as Possible; The Psychological impact of incarceration and How to Maintain Your MAXIMUM Level of Mental Health; Prison Art Techniques; Fulfilling Food Recipes; Parole Preparation Strategies and much, MUCH more!

GET OUT, STAY OUT!, $16.95 & $5.00 S/H: This book should be in the hands of everyone in a prison cell. It reveals a challenging but clear course for overcoming the obstacles that stand between prisoners and their freedom. For those behind bars, one goal outshines all others: GETTING OUT! After being released, that goal then shifts to STAYING OUT! This book will help prisoners do both. It has been masterfully constructed into five parts that will help prisoners maximize focus while they strive to accomplish whichever goal is at hand.

MOB$TAR MONEY, $12.00 & $4.00 S/H: After Trey's mother is sent to prison for 75 years to life, he and his little brother are moved from their home in Sacramento, California, to his grandmother's house in Stockton, California where he is forced to find his way in life and become a man on his own in the city's grimy streets. One day, on his way home from the local corner store, Trey has a rough encounter with the neighborhood bully. Luckily, that's when Tyson, a member of the MOBTAR, a local "get money" gang comes to his aid. The two kids quickly become friends, and it doesn't take long before Trey is embraced into the notorious MOB$TAR money gang, which opens the door to an adventure full of sex, money, murder and mayhem that will change his life forever... You will never guess how this story ends!

BLOCK MONEY, $12.00 & $4.00 S/H: Beast, a young thug from the grimy streets of central Stockton, California lives The Block; breathes The Block; and has committed himself to bleed The Block for all it's worth until his very last breath. Then, one day, he meets Nadia; a stripper at the local club who piques his curiosity with her beauty, quick-witted intellect and rider qualities. The problem? She has a man – Esco – a local kingpin with money and power. It doesn't take long, however, before a devious plot is hatched to pull off a heist worth an indeterminable amount of money. Following the acts of treachery, deception and betrayal are twists and turns and a bloody war that will leave you speechless!

HOW TO HUSTLE & WIN: SEX, MONEY, MURDER EDITION $15.00 & $5.00 S/H: *How To Hu$tle & Win: Sex, Money, Murder Edition* is the grittiest, underground self-help manual for the 21st century street entrepreneur in print. Never has there been such a book written for today's gangsters, goons and go-getters. This self-help handbook is an absolute must-have for anyone who is actively connected to the streets.

RAW LAW: YOUR RIGHTS, & HOW TO SUE WHEN THEY ARE VIOLATED! $15.00 & $5.00 S/H: *Raw Law For Prisoners* is a clear and concise guide for prisoners and their advocates to understanding civil rights laws guaranteed to prisoners under the US Constitution, and how to successfully file a lawsuit when those rights have been violated! From initial complaint to trial, this book will take you through the entire process, step by step, in simple, easy-to-understand terms. Also included are several examples where prisoners have sued prison officials successfully, resulting in changes of unjust rules and regulations and recourse for rights violations, oftentimes resulting in rewards of thousands, even millions of dollars in damages! If you feel your rights have been violated, don't lash out at guards, which is usually ineffective and only makes matters worse. Instead, defend yourself successfully by using the legal system, and getting the power of the courts on your side!

HOW TO WRITE URBAN BOOKS FOR MONEY & FAME: $16.95 & $5.00 S/H: Inside this book you will learn the true story of how Mike

Enemigo and King Guru have received money and fame from inside their prison cells by writing urban books; the secrets to writing hood classics so you, too, can be caked up and famous; proper punctuation using hood examples; and resources you can use to achieve your money motivated ambitions! If you're a prisoner who want to write urban novels for money and fame, this must-have manual will give you all the game!

PRETTY GIRLS LOVE BAD BOYS: AN INMATE'S GUIDE TO GETTING GIRLS: $15.00 & $5.00 S/H: Tired of the same, boring, cliché pen pal books that don't tell you what you really need to know? If so, this book is for you! Anything you need to know on the art of long and short distance seduction is included within these pages! Not only does it give you the science of attracting pen pals from websites, it also includes psychological profiles and instructions on how to seduce any woman you set your sights on! Includes interviews of women who have fallen in love with prisoners, bios for pen pal ads, pre-written love letters, romantic poems, love-song lyrics, jokes and much, much more! This book is the ultimate guide – a must-have for any prisoner who refuses to let prison walls affect their MAC'n.

THE LADIES WHO LOVE PRISONERS, $15.00 & $5.00 S/H: New Special Report reveals the secrets of real women who have fallen in love with prisoners, regardless of crime, sentence, or location. This info will give you a HUGE advantage in getting girls from prison.

THE MILLIONAIRE PRISONER: PART 1, $16.95 & $5.00 S/H

THE MILLIONAIRE PRISONER: PART 2, $16.95 & $5.00 S/H

THE MILLIONAIRE PRISONER: SPECIAL 2-IN-1 EDITION, $24.99 & $7.00 S/H: Why wait until you get out of prison to achieve your dreams? Here's a blueprint that you can use to become successful! *The Millionaire Prisoner* is your complete reference to overcoming any obstacle in prison. You won't be able to put it down! With this book you will discover the secrets to: Making money from your cell! Obtain FREE money for correspondence courses! Become an expert on any topic! Develop the habits of the rich! Network with celebrities! Set up your own website! Market your products, ideas and services! Successfully use prison pen pal websites! All of this and much, much more! This book has enabled thousands of prisoners to succeed and it will show you the way also!

THE MILLIONAIRE PRISONER 3: SUCCESS UNIVERSITY, $16.95 & $5 S/H: Why wait until you get out of prison to achieve your dreams? Here's a new-look blueprint that you can use to be successful! *The Millionaire Prisoner 3* contains advanced strategies to overcoming any obstacle in prison. You won't be able to put it down!

THE MILLIONAIRE PRISONER 4: PEN PAL MASTERY, $16.95 & $5.00 S/H: Tired of subpar results? Here's a master blueprint that you can use to get tons of pen pals! *TMP 4: Pen Pal Mastery* is your complete roadmap to finding your one true love. You won't be able to put it down! With this book you'll DISCOVER the SECRETS to: Get FREE pen pals & which sites are best to use; Successful tactics female prisoners can win with; Use astrology to find love; friendship & more; Build a winning social media presence; Playing phone tag & successful sex talk; Hidden benefits of foreign pen pals; Find your success mentors; Turning "hits" into friendships; Learn how to write letters/emails that get results. All of this and much more!

GET OUT, GET RICH: HOW TO GET PAID LEGALLY WHEN YOU GET OUT OF PRISON!, $16.95 & $5.00 S/H: Many of you are incarcerated for a money-motivated crime. But with today's tech and opportunities, not only is the crime-for-money risk/reward ratio not strategically wise, it's not even necessary. You can earn much more money by partaking in any one of the easy, legal hustles explained in this book, regardless of your record. Help yourself earn an honest income so you can not only make a lot of money, but say good-bye to penitentiary chances and prison forever! (Note: Many things in this book can even he done from inside prison.) (ALSO PUBLISHED AS *HOOD MILLIONAIRE: HOW TO HUSTLE AND WIN LEGALLY!*)

THE CEO MANUAL: HOW TO START A BUSINESS WHEN YOU GET OUT OF PRISON, $16.95 & $5.00 S/H: $16.95 & $5 S/H: This new book will teach you the simplest way to start your own business when you get out of prison. Includes: Start-up Steps! The Secrets to Pulling Money from Investors! How to Manage People Effectively! How To Legally Protect Your Assets from "them"! Hundreds of resources to get you started, including a list of "loan friendly" banks! (ALSO PUBLISHED AS *CEO MANUAL: START A BUSINESS, BE A BOSS!*)

THE MONEY MANUAL: UNDERGROUND CASH SECRETS EXPOSED! 16.95 & $5.00 S/H: Becoming a millionaire is equal parts what you make, and what you don't spend – AKA save. All Millionaires and Billionaires have mastered the art of not only making money, but keeping the money they make (remember Donald Trump's tax maneuvers?), as well as establishing credit so that they are loaned money by banks and trusted with money from investors: AKA OPM – other people's money. And did you know there are millionaires and billionaires just waiting to GIVE money away? It's true! These are all very-little known secrets "they" don't want YOU to know about, but that I'm exposing in my new book!

HOOD MILLIONAIRE; HOW TO HUSTLE & WIN LEGALLY, $16.95 & $5.00 S/H: Hustlin' is a way of life in the hood. We all have money motivated ambitions, not only because we gotta eat, but because status is oftentimes determined by one's own salary. To achieve what we consider financial success, we often invest our efforts into illicit activities – we take penitentiary chances. This leads to a life in and out of prison, sometimes death – both of which are counterproductive to gettin' money. But there's a solution to this, and I have it...

CEO MANUAL: START A BUSINESS BE A BOSS, $16.95 & $5.00 S/H: After the success of the urban-entrepreneur classic *Hood Millionaire: How To Hustle & Win Legally!*, self-made millionaires Mike Enemigo and Sav Hustle team back up to bring you the latest edition of the Hood Millionaire series – *CEO Manual: Start A Business, Be A Boss!* In this latest collection of game laying down the art of "hoodpreneurship", you will learn such things as: 5 Core Steps to Starting Your Own Business! 5 Common Launch Errors You Must Avoid! How To

Write a Business Plan! How To Legally Protect Your Assets From "Them"! How To Make Your Business Fundable, Where to Get Money for Your Start-up Business, and even How to Start a Business With No Money! You will learn How to Drive Customers to Your Website, How to Maximize Marketing Dollars, Contract Secrets for the savvy boss, and much, much more! And as an added bonus, we have included over 200 Business Resources, from government agencies and small business development centers, to a secret list of small-business friendly banks that will help you get started!

PAID IN FULL: WELCOME TO DA GAME, $15.00 & $5.00 S/H. In 1983, the movie *Scarface* inspired many kids growing up in America's inner cities to turn their rags into riches by becoming cocaine kingpins. Harlem's Azie Faison was one of them. Faison would ultimately connect with Harlem's Rich Porter and Alpo Martinez, and the trio would go on to become certified street legends of the '80s and early '90s. Years later, Dame Dash and Roc-A-Fella Films would tell their story in the based-on-actual-events movie, *Paid in Full*. But now, we are telling the story our way – The Cell Block way – where you will get a perspective of the story that the movie did not show, ultimately learning an outcome that you did not expect. Book one of our series, *Paid in Full: Welcome to da Game*, will give you an inside look at a key player in this story, one that is not often talked about – Lulu, the Columbian cocaine kingpin with direct ties to Pablo Escobar, who plugged Azie in with an unlimited amount of top-tier cocaine at dirt-cheap prices that helped boost the trio to neighborhood superstars and certified kingpin status... until greed, betrayal, and murder destroyed everything....

OJ'S LIFE BEHIND BARS, $15.00 & $5 S/H: In 1994, Heisman Trophy winner and NFL superstar OJ Simpson was arrested for the brutal murder of his ex-wife Nicole Brown-Simpson and her friend Ron Goldman. In 1995, after the "trial of the century," he was acquitted of both murders, though most of the world believes he did it. In 2007 OJ was again arrested, but this time in Las Vegas, for armed robbery and kidnapping. On October 3, 2008 he was found guilty sentenced to 33 years and was sent to Lovelock Correctional Facility, in Lovelock, Nevada. There he met inmate-author Vernon Nelson. Vernon was granted a true, insider's perspective into the mind and life of one of the country's most notorious men; one that has never been provided...until now.

BLINDED BY BETRAYAL, $15.00 & $5.00 S/H. Khalil wanted nothing more than to chase his rap dream when he got out of prison. After all, a fellow inmate had connected him with a major record producer that could help him take his career to unimaginable heights, and his girl is in full support of his desire to trade in his gun for a mic. Problem is, Khalil's crew, the notorious Blood Money Squad, awaited him with open arms, unaware of his desire to leave the game alone, and expected him to jump head first into the life of fast money and murder. Will Khalil be able to balance his desire to get out of the game with the expectations of his gang to participate in it? Will he be able to pull away before it's too late? Or, will the streets pull him right back in, ultimately causing his demise? One thing for sure, the streets are loyal to no one, and blood money comes with bloody consequences....

THE MOB, $16.99 & $5 S/H. PaperBoy is a Bay Area boss who has invested blood, sweat, and years into building The Mob – a network of Bay Area Street legends, block bleeders, and underground rappers who collaborate nationwide in the interest of pushing a multi-million-dollar criminal enterprise of sex, drugs, and murder.

Based on actual events, little has been known about PaperBoy, the mastermind behind The Mob, and intricate details of its operation, until now.

Follow this story to learn about some of the Bay Area underworld's most glamorous figures and famous events...

AOB, $15.00 & $5 S/H. Growing up in the Bay Area, Manny Fresh the Best had a front-row seat to some of the coldest players to ever do it. And you already know, A.O.B. is the name of the Game! So, When Manny Fresh slides through Stockton one day and sees Rosa, a stupid-bad Mexican chick with a whole lotta 'talent' behind her walking down the street tryna get some money, he knew immediately what he had to do: Put it In My Pocket!

AOB 2, $15.00 & $5 S/H.

AOB 3, $15.00 & $5 S/H

PIMPOLOGY: THE 7 ISMS OF THE GAME, $15.00 & $5 S/H: It's been said that if you knew better, you'd do better. So, in the spirit of dropping jewels upon the rare few who truly want to know how to win, this collection of exclusive Game has been compiled. And though a lot of so-called players claim to know how the Pimp Game is supposed to go, none have revealed the real. . . Until now!

JAILHOUSE PUBLISHING FOR MONEY, POWER & FAME: $24.99 & $7 S/H: In 2010, after flirting with the idea for two years, Mike Enemigo started writing his first book. In 2014, he officially launched his publishing company, The Cell Block, with the release of five books. Of course, with no mentor(s), how-to guides, or any real resources, he was met with failure after failure as he tried to navigate the treacherous goal of publishing books from his prison cell. However, he was determined to make it. He was determined to figure it out and he refused to quit. In Mike's new book, *Jailhouse Publishing for Money, Power, and Fame,* he breaks down all his jailhouse publishing secrets and strategies, so you can do all he's done, but without the trials and tribulations he's had to go through...

KITTY KAT, ADULT ENTERTAINMENT RESOURCE BOOK, $24.99 & $9.00 S/H: This book is jam packed with hundreds of sexy non nude photos including photo spreads. The book contains the complete info on sexy photo sellers, hot magazines, page turning bookstore, sections on strip clubs, porn stars, alluring models, thought provoking stories and must-see movies.

PRISON LEGAL GUIDE, $24.99 & $9.00 S/H: The laws of the U.S. Judicial system are complex, complicated, and always growing and changing. Many prisoners spend days on end digging through its intricacies. Pile on top of the legal code the rules and regulations of a correctional facility, and you can see how high the deck is being stacked against you. Correct legal information is the key to your survival when you have run afoul of the system (or it is running afoul of you). Whether you are an accomplished jailhouse lawyer helping newbies learn the ropes, an old head fighting bare-knuckle for your rights in the courts, or a hustler just looking to beat the latest write-up – this book has something for you!

**PRISON HEALTH HANDBOOK, $19.99 &
$9.00 S/H:** The Prison Health Handbook is your one-stop go-to source for information on how to maintain your best health while inside the American prison system. Filled with information, tips, and secrets from doctors, gurus, and other experts, this book will educate you on such things as proper workout and exercise regimens; yoga benefits for prisoners; how to meditate effectively; pain management tips; sensible dieting solutions; nutritional knowledge; an understanding of various cancers, diabetes, hepatitis, and other diseases all too common in prison; how to effectively deal with mental health issues such as stress, PTSD, anxiety, and depression; a list of things your doctors DON'T want YOU to know; and much, much more!

All books are available on thecellblock.net.

You can also order by sending a money order or institutional check to:

The Cell Block
PO Box 1025
Rancho Cordova, CA 95741

PRISON RIOT RADIO

Industry reps want to hear you!

Are you a rapper? We will upload your freestyles to our website, prisonriotradio.com, FREE for top industry execs to hear!

Pick up the phone and become a star!

We will record you on the phone! All raw freestyles will be recorded FREE. If you need a recording and a beat, the prices are below...

$25 Per Recording

$150 For 8 Recordings

$30 Per Beat

$10 For Cover Art

We accept songs, spoken word, podcasts and interviews! Learn the game and how to get your money!

For more information, to send material, or to set up a phone recording session, email prisonriotradio@gmail.com or jayrene@prisonriotradio@gmail.com.